DAILY LIFE
IN
BIBLE TIMES

DAILY LIFE
IN
BIBLE TIMES

Edited by

JAMES I. PACKER, A.M., D.PHIL.
Regent College

MERRILL C. TENNEY, A.M., Ph.D.
Wheaton Graduate School

WILLIAM WHITE, JR., Th.M., Ph.D.

THOMAS NELSON PUBLISHERS
Nashville • Camden • New York

Published in Nashville, Tennessee, by Thomas Nelson, Inc., Publishers and distributed in Canada by Lawson Falle, Ltd., Cambridge, Ontario.

Printed in the United States of America.

Library of Congress Cataloging in Publication Data

Packer, J. I. (James Innell)
  Daily life in Bible times.

  Includes index.
  1. Sociology, Biblical.   2. Jews—Social life and customs.   3. Jews—
History—To 70 A.D.
I. Tenney, Merrill Chapin, 1904-   II. White, William,
1934-   .   III. Title.
BS670.P32   1982   220.9'5   82-12618
ISBN 0-8407-5822-7

INTRODUCTION

Daily Life in Bible Times presents the results of the latest Biblical and archaeological research regarding the everyday life and practices of the people of the Bible. The laws, customs, and habits of Bible times are very different from those of our own day; and when we are able to understand these differences, we will have a much clearer picture of many of the events recorded in the Bible.

The family life described in the Scriptures is quite distinct from our own. Women and children occupied different places in society than they do in our age. Furthermore, in Bible times the women of Israel enjoyed a much more favorable status than did the women of the surrounding cultures. The high concept of marriage that the Hebrews held was unique in that time, even though there was a constant tension between Israel's ideals and the corrupt practices of the people among whom they lived. Children were welcomed into the family, and in a number of instances the biblical family's love for children is reflected in the Scriptures. Another element of family life that was quite different from our own is the high degree of respect that was paid to the elderly.

Daily Life in Bible Times is about much more than family life. Sickness and healing, food and eating habits, and clothing and dress are also discussed in a way designed to aid the reader of the Bible to picture the practices of the biblical era.

Compared to the Romans and Greeks, Hebrew architecture was simple. In the earliest times the people lived in large tents, and only as Israel became more settled were homes built and the differences between the wealthy and the poor made obvious. Israel's music was simple, too, although eventually instruments were introduced from the people who surrounded the nation. In addition, David is credited with inventing several musical instruments. Many of these instruments were used in worship.

Israel's worship was marked by awe and thanksgiving, hope and gratitude. Even though this worship was not always faithful, Israel did experience the blessings of God's promises. It was this confident hope that brought such exuberant joy to their celebrations.

Daily Life in Bible Times is a guidebook to the laws, customs, and mores of the biblical period. The student of the Bible is encouraged to read it and to discover their significance in Israel's life, as well as their significance for today.

TABLE OF CONTENTS

1

FAMILY RELATIONSHIPS

Two facts stand out in what the Bible says about the family and its relationships. First, the roles of family members stayed about the same throughout the biblical period. Changing culture and laws did not affect family customs to any great extent. It is true that the folks who lived in the early days of the Old Testament period were semi-nomadic—they often moved from one area to another—so their habits were different from those of settled peoples in some ways. The Mosaic Law abolished some of the nomadic practices, such as marrying one's sister. But most of the original family life-style persisted, even into the New Testament era.

Second, family life in Bible times reflected a culture quite different from our own. We should recognize this difference when we turn to the Scriptures for guidance in raising our own families. We should search out the principles of Scripture rather than directly copy the specific life-styles it portrays. These life-styles were designed for small agricultural communities, and they did not please God in every case.

As an example, the culture of that day allowed a man to have more than one wife, and some men of God did; yet nowhere does Scripture state that God approved this practice. We classify it as a tolerated cultural custom, but not a biblically prescribed one.

Another instance: When Abraham lived in Egypt with Sarah, he told her to say she was his sister, fearing that the Egyptians would kill him because of her great beauty. She was in fact his half-sister, a degree of kinship that God later specified as too close for marriage (cf. Gen. 20:12; Lev. 18:9). As a result, the pharaoh took Sarah into his house and God afflicted the pharaoh's family with plagues in order to rescue her.

The biblical teaching for family life includes instructions for children, mothers, and fathers. We will see examples of families that followed God's wishes and were greatly blessed; we will also see families that disobeyed God and reaped the consequences. Along the way we will notice how family life changed during the course of Israel's history.

THE FAMILY UNIT

The family was the first social structure that God produced. He formed the first family by joining Adam and Eve together as husband and wife (Gen. 2:18-24). The man and woman became the nucleus of a family unit.

Why did God create the family structure? Genesis 2:18 says that God created the woman as a helper for Adam, which indicates that the man and woman were brought together first for companionship; the wife was to help her husband, and the husband was to care for his wife. Then the two together were to meet the needs of their children, the offspring of their relationship.

A. Husband. The Hebrew word for *husband* partially means "to dominate, to rule." It can also be translated as "master." As head of the family, the husband was responsible for its well-being. For example, when Abraham and Sarah deceived the pharaoh about their marriage, the ruler challenged Abraham rather than Sarah, who had done the actual lying (Gen. 12:17-20). This does not mean that the Hebrew husband was a tyrant who enjoyed bossing his family around. Rather, he lovingly assumed responsibility for the family and sought to serve the needs of those who were under his authority.

Every Jewish couple married with the idea of having children. They were especially eager to have a male child. A man fortunate enough to father a son was proud indeed. Jeremiah noted, "The man who brought tidings to my father, saying, a man child is born unto thee; [made] him very glad" (Jer. 20:15).

The Jewish father assumed spiritual leadership within the family; he functioned as the family priest (cf. Gen. 12:8; Job 1:5). He was expected to lead his family in observing various religious rites, such as the Passover (Exod. 12:3).

Along with the wife, the father was to "train up a child in the way he should go . . ." (Prov. 22:6). The father also had to convey all of the written law to his children. The father was admonished to "teach them diligently unto thy children, and shalt talk of them when thou sittest in thine house, and when thou walkest by the way, and when thou liest down, and when thou risest up. And thou shalt bind them for a sign upon thine hand, and they shall be as frontlets between thine eyes. And thou shalt write them on the posts of thy house, and on thy gates" (Deut. 6:7-9).

Reconstructed Old Testament house. The reconstructed interior of a typical house in biblical times shows the cooking stove (to the left of the center) and a water jug with dipper (foreground). A horizontal loom hangs from a pole on the lefthand side in the family's eating area—a circular mat set with bowls. Storage jars, baskets, and bowls sit on shelves, benches, and the floor.

At the city gate. The city gates were centers for conversations and commerce. Gates were often named for the items traded there (e.g., Sheep Gate, Fish Gate). Because the elders often transacted business at the gate, to "sit at the gate" meant to attain a certain social eminence.

The father had to inflict physical punishment when necessary. This was to be done in such a way as not to "provoke your children to wrath: but bring them up in the nurture and admonition of the Lord" (Eph. 6:4).

In biblical times, a man who did not provide adequately for his family was guilty of a serious offense. A man who failed to do this was shunned and mocked by society (cf. Prov. 6:6-11; 19:7). Paul wrote, "If any provide not for his own, . . . he hath denied the faith, and is worse than an infidel" (1 Tim. 5:8).

As husband and father, the man defended his family's rights before the judges when necessary (see Deut. 22:13-19). "The fatherless and the widow" had no man to defend their rights, so they were often denied justice (cf. Deut. 10:18).

The Jewish people were governed by various Jewish traditions. The Talmud says that a father had four responsibilities toward his son, besides teaching him the Law. He must circumcise his son (cf. Gen. 17:12-13), redeem him from God if he were the firstborn (cf. Num. 18:15-16), find him a wife (cf. Gen. 24:4), and teach him a trade.

A good father thought of his children as full human beings, and took note of their feelings and abilities. A Jewish scholar of the time said that a good father should "push them away with the left hand and draw them near with the right hand." This delicate balance between firmness and affection typified the ideal Jewish father.

B. Wife. In marriage, the woman willingly took a place of submission to her mate. The wife's responsibility was to be the husband's "helpmeet" (Gen. 2:18, RSV), one who "does him good, and not harm, all the days of her life" (Prov. 31:12). Her main responsibility centered around the home and the children, but sometimes it extended to the marketplace and other areas that affected the family's welfare (cf. Prov. 31:16, 25).

A wife's primary goal in life was to bear children for her husband. Rebekah's family spokesman said to her, "Thou art our sister, be thou the mother of thousands of millions and let thy seed possess the gate of those who hate them" (Gen. 24:60). A Jewish family hoped that the wife would become like a fruitful vine, filling the house with many children (Psa. 128:3). So a mother greeted the first child with much happiness and relief.

As children began to arrive, the mother was tied closer to the home. She nursed each child until the age of two or three, besides clothing and feeding the rest of the family. She spent hours each day preparing meals and making clothes from wool. When necessary, the wife helped her husband in the fields, planting or harvesting the crops.

A mother shared the responsibility for training the children. Children spent the early formative years close to their mothers. Eventually, the sons were old enough to go with their fathers into the fields or some other place of employment (cf. Prov. 31:1-9). The mother then turned her attention more fully to her daughters, teaching them how to become successful wives and mothers.

A woman's performance of her tasks determined the failure

or success of the family. The wise men said, "A virtuous woman is the crown to her husband, but she that maketh ashamed is as rottenness in his bones" (Prov. 12:4). If the wife worked hard at the task laid before her, it greatly benefited her husband. Jews believed that a man could rise to a place among the leaders of Israel only if his wife were wise and talented (cf. Prov. 31:23).

C. Sons. In biblical times, the sons had to support their parents when they became old and then give them a proper burial. For this reason, a couple usually hoped to have many sons. "As arrows are in the hand of a mighty man; so are children of the youth. Happy is the man that hath his quiver full of them: they shall not be ashamed, but they shall speak with the enemies in the gate" (Psa. 127:4-5).

The firstborn son held a very special place of honor within the family. He was expected to be the next head of the family. All through his life, he was expected to take greater responsibility for his actions and the actions of his brothers. This was why Reuben, as the oldest brother, showed greater concern for the life of Joseph, when his brothers agreed to kill him (Gen. 37:21, 29).

When the father died, a firstborn son received a double portion of the family inheritance (Deut. 21:17; 2 Chron. 21:2-3).

The fifth commandment admonished, "Honor thy father and thy mother; that thy days may be long upon the land which the Lord thy God giveth thee" (Exod. 20:12). Both parents were to receive the same amount of respect. However, the rabbis of the Talmud reasoned that if a son ever had to choose, he must give preference to his father. For example, if both parents requested a drink of water simultaneously, the Talmud taught that both the son and the mother should meet the needs of the father.

Jesus was the perfect example of an obedient son. Luke noted that at the age of 12, Jesus "went down with them and came to Nazareth, and was subject to them" (Luke 2:51). Even while enduring the agonies of the cross, Jesus thought of His mother and His responsibility toward her as the firstborn son.

He asked John to care for her after His death, thereby fulfilling His duty out of love (John 19:27).

D. Daughters. In ancient times, daughters were not prized as highly as sons. Some fathers actually looked upon them as a nuisance. For example, one father wrote, "The father waketh for the daughter, when no man knoweth; and the care for her taketh away sleep: when she is young, lest she pass away the flower of her age [fail to marry]; and being married, lest she should be hated; in her virginity, lest she should be defiled and gotten with child become pregnant in her father's house; or having an husband, lest she should misbehave herself; and when she is married, lest she should be barren" (Ecclesiasticus 42:9-10).

However, the Hebrews treated their daughters more hu-

Grinding meal, baking bread. The Hebrews used stones to grind wheat and barley into flour. They kneaded flour, yeast, olive oil, and water or milk into a dough that was stretched thin for baking.

manely than some of the surrounding cultures. The Romans actually exposed newborn girls to the elements, in the hope that they would die. The Hebrews believed that all life—male and female—came from God. For this reason, they would never consider killing one of their babies. In fact, when the prophet Nathan sought to describe the intimate relationship of a father to a child, he pictured a *daughter* in her father's arms with her head on his chest (2 Sam. 12:3).

Firstborn daughters held a special place of honor and duty within the family. For example, Lot's firstborn daughter tried to persuade her younger sister to bear a child for Lot, to preserve the family (Gen. 19:31-38). In the story of Laban and Jacob, the firstborn daughter Leah was given priority over the younger sister (Gen. 29:26).

If a family was without sons, the daughters could inherit their father's possessions (Num. 27:5-8); but they could keep their inheritance only if they married within their own tribe (Num. 36:5-12).

The daughter was under the legal dominion of her father until her marriage. Her father made all important decisions for her, such as whom she should marry. But the daughter was asked to give her consent to the choice of a groom, and sometimes she was even allowed to state a preference (Gen. 24:58; 1 Sam. 18:20). The father approved all vows the daughter made before they became binding (Num. 30:1-5).

A Jewish "Table." An Israelite family of Old Testament times would have eaten around a floor mat like this one, where the simple clay dishes were set. This reconstruction is in the Ha-Aretz Museum in Tel Aviv.

The daughter was expected to help her mother in the home. At a very early age, she began to learn the various domestic skills she needed to become a good wife and mother herself. By the age of 12, the daughter had become a homemaker in her own right and was allowed to marry.

In some Near Eastern cultures, families did not allow their daughters to leave the home. If they did appear in public, they had to wear a veil over their faces and were not allowed to speak to a male. The Israelites placed no such restrictions on their daughters. Girls were relatively free to come and go, provided their work was done. We see examples of this in Rebekah, who talked to a stranger at the well (Gen. 24:15-21), and the seven daughters of the priests of Midian, who chatted with Moses as they watered their father's flock (Exod. 2:16-22).

Young ladies in biblical times were very concerned about their appearance. They believed that light skin was beautiful. If a young woman became tanned by the sun, she hid from public view (Song of Sol. 1:6). For this reason, women tried to do their outdoor work in the early morning or the late afternoon. Sometimes, though, a woman was forced out into the noonday sun, as was the girl in the Song of Solomon. She accused her brothers of making her the "keeper of the vineyards," which meant that she had to be outdoors most of the day (Song of Sol. 1:6).

The family expected a daughter to remain a virgin until her marriage. Unfortunately, this did not always happen. Some young women were seduced or raped. When this happened, the Mosaic Law made careful distinctions between the punishment for raping girls who were engaged and those who were not.

Often daughters married at an early age. Such early marriages did not create the problems that they do today. Though a bride left the dominion of her father, she entered the new domain of her husband and his family. Her mother-in-law stepped in to continue the guidance and training her own mother had given her. The wife and her mother-in-law often developed a deep and lasting bond. This is perfectly illustrated in the Book of Ruth, when Naomi repeatedly refers to Ruth as "my daughter." Micah described a strife-filled family as one in which "the daughter riseth up against her mother, the daughter-in-law against her mother-in-law" (Mic. 7:6).

When a young woman went to live with her husband's family, she did not give up all rights in her own family. If her husband died and there were no more brothers-in-law for her to marry, she might return to her father's house. That is exactly what Naomi encouraged her daughters-in-law to do, and Orpah followed her suggestion (Ruth 1:8-18).

E. Brothers and Sisters. Love developed between brothers as they grew up together, sharing responsibilities, problems, and victories. One of the Proverbs states, "A man that hath friends must show himself friendly, and there is a friend that sticketh closer than a brother" (Prov. 18:24).

Joseph displayed real love toward his brothers. But while he was young, his brothers sold him into slavery because they hated their father's favoritism toward him. Later, when Joseph gained power and position, he could have evened the score with his brothers. Instead, he showed them love and mercy. He said, "Now therefore be not grieved, nor angry with yourselves, that ye sold me hither: for God did send me before you to preserve life" (Gen. 45:5).

The Bible describes many brothers who maintained a deep and abiding love for one another. The Psalmist described the love of brothers by saying, "It is like the precious oil upon the head, that ran down upon the beard, upon even Aaron's beard, that went to the skirts of his garments; as the dew of Hermon . . . that descended the mountains of Zion!" (Psa. 133:2-3, RSV).

Brothers and sisters also shared a special bond. Job's sons would never have entertained without inviting their 3 sisters (Job 1:4). When Dinah was raped, her brothers avenged the crime (Gen. 34).

In earlier times, young men sometimes married their half sisters. Both Abraham and Sarah had the same father but different mothers (Gen. 20:12). As we have already noted, the Mosaic Law banned this practice (Lev. 18:9; 20:17; Deut. 27:22).

The bond of love between sisters and brothers was so strong that the Mosaic Law allowed even a priest to touch the body of a dead brother, sister, parent, or child (Lev. 21:1-3). This was the only time that a priest could touch a dead person and not become unceremonially clean.

THE EXTENDED FAMILY

In the most basic sense, a Hebrew family consisted of a husband, a wife, and their children. When the husband had more than one wife, the "family" included all of the wives and the children in their various relationships (cf. Gen. 30). Sometimes the family included everyone who shared a common dwelling place under the protection of the head of the family. They might be grandparents, servants, and visitors, as well as widowed daughters and their children. The extended family commonly included sons and their wives and children (Lev. 18:6-18). God counted Abraham's slaves as part of the family group, for He required Abraham to circumcise them (Gen. 17:12-14, 22-27). In Israel's early history, as many as four generations lived together. This was a normal part of the semi-nomadic life-style and the later agricultural one.

Even today in the Middle East, semi-nomadic people band together as large families for the sake of survival. Each extended family has its own "father" or *sheik,* whose word is law.

In Old Testament days, the extended family was ruled by the oldest male in the household, who was also called the "father." Often this person was a grandfather or a great-grandfather. For example, when Jacob's family moved to Egypt, Jacob was considered their "father"—even though his sons had wives and families (cf. Gen. 46:8-27). Jacob continued to rule over his "family" until his death.

The "father" of an extended family held the power of life and death over all of its members. We see this when Abraham nearly sacrificed his son, Isaac (Gen. 22:9-12), and when Judah sentenced his daughter-in-law to death because she had committed adultery (Gen. 38:24-26).

Later, the Mosaic Law restricted the father's authority. It did not allow him to sacrifice his child on an altar (Lev. 18:21). It allowed him to sell his daughter, but not to a foreigner and not for prostitution (Exod. 21:7; Lev. 19:29). According to the law, a father could not deny the birthright of his firstborn son, even if he had sons by two different women (Deut. 21:15-17).

Some Hebrew fathers violated these laws, as in the case of Jephthah, who vowed to sacrifice whoever came out to greet him upon his victorious return from battle. His daughter was the first. Believing that he had to keep his vow, Jephthah sacrificed her (Judg. 11:31, 34-40). Likewise, King Manasseh burned his son to appease a heathen god (2 Kings 21:6).

We do not know when the extended family of Old Testament times gave way to the family structure we know today. Some scholars feel that it died out during the monarchy of David and Solomon. Others believe that it continued longer than that. But by New Testament times, the extended family had all but disappeared. Paul's writings confirm this; when he wrote about the roles and attitudes of each family member, he spoke only of parents, children and slaves (cf. Eph. 5:21-6:9).

The New Testament says that Joseph and Mary traveled as a couple to be taxed at Bethlehem (Luke 2:4-5). They went to the temple alone when Mary offered her sacrifices (Luke 2:22). They also traveled alone when they took Jesus into Egypt (Matt. 2:14). These accounts tend to confirm that the "family" of the New Testament consisted only of the husband, wife, and children.

THE CLAN

The extended family was part of a larger group that we call a *clan*. The clan might be so large that it registered hundreds of males in its ranks (cf. Gen. 46:8-27; Ezra 8:1-14). Members of a clan shared a common ancestry, and thus viewed each other as kinsmen. They felt obligated to help and protect one another.

Often the clan designated one male, called a *goel*, to extend help to clan members in need. In English, this person is referred to as the *kinsman-redeemer*. His help covered many areas of need.

If a member of the clan had to sell part of his property to pay debts, he gave the kinsman-redeemer the first opportunity to purchase it. The kinsman-redeemer then had to purchase the property, if he could, to keep it in the clan's possession (Lev. 25:25; cf. Ruth 4:1-6). This situation arose when Jeremiah's cousin came to him, saying, "Buy thee my field. . .that is in Anathoth, for the right of redemption is thine. . .buy it for thyself" (Jer. 32:6-8). Jeremiah purchased the field and used the event to proclaim that the Jews would eventually return to Israel (Jer. 32:15).

Occasionally, an army would capture hostages and sell them to the highest bidder. Also, a man might sell himself into slavery to repay a debt. In both cases, the slave's next-of-kin had to find the clan's kinsman-redeemer, who would try to purchase his kinsman's freedom (Lev. 25:47-49).

If a married man died without having had a child, the *goel* had to marry the widow (Deut. 25:5-10). This was called a *levirate* ("brother-in-law") marriage. Any children born through this arrangement were considered the offspring of the deceased brother.

The story of Ruth and Naomi well illustrates the responsibility of the kinsman-redeemer. The widow Naomi had to sell her property near Bethlehem, and she wanted her childless daughter-in-law to remarry. The nearest of kin agreed to purchase the field but was unwilling to marry Ruth. So he gave up both obligations in a ceremony conducted before the elders of the city. Then Boaz, the next nearest-of-kin, bought the field and married Ruth (Ruth 4:9-10).

A *goel* had to avenge a kinsman's murder. In such a case, he was called the "avenger of blood" (cf. Deut. 19:12). The law of Moses limited this practice by establishing cities of refuge where killers could flee, but even this did not insure the killer's safety. If the murder was done out of malice or forethought, the avenger of blood would follow him to the city of refuge and demand his return. In such a case, the murderer would be turned over to the *goel,* who would kill him (cf. Deut. 19:1-13). Joab killed Abner in this manner (2 Sam. 2:22-23).

EROSION OF THE FAMILY

A family that lives in harmony and in genuine love is a delight to all associated with it. Surely this is what God had in mind when He established the family. Unfortunately, the Bible shows us few families that attained this ideal. Throughout Bible history, families were being eroded by social, economic, and religious pressures. We can identify several of these pressures.

A. Childlessness. Childlessness was a major threat to a marriage in biblical times. If a couple was unable to conceive a child, they looked upon their problem as a chastisement from God.

In spite of his continued love for his wife, a childless man sometimes married a second woman or used the services of a slave to conceive children (Gen. 16:2; 30:3; Deut. 21:10-14). Some men divorced their wives in order to do this. While this practice solved the problem of childlessness, it created many other problems.

B. Polygamy. There was continuous domestic strife when two women shared a husband in Old Testament times. The Hebrew word for the second wife literally meant "rival wife" (cf. 1 Sam. 1:6); this suggests that bitterness and hostility usually existed between polygamous wives. Nevertheless, polygamy was customary, especially in the time of the patriarchs. If a man was unable to raise the marriage money for a second wife, he considered buying a slave for that purpose or using one he already had in his household (cf. Gen. 16:2; 30:3-8).

In a polygamous marriage, the husband invariably favored one wife over another. This caused complications, such as deciding whose child to honor as firstborn son. Sometimes a man wanted to give his inheritance to the son of his favored wife although it was actually owed to the son of the "disliked" wife (Deut. 21:15-17). Moses declared that the firstborn son had to be rightfully honored, and the husband could not shortchange the firstborn's mother to "diminish her food, her clothing, or her marital right" (Exod. 21:10).

Politics was also a motive for polygamy. Often a king sealed a covenant with another king by marrying his ally's daughter. When Scripture speaks of Solomon's large harem, it points out that "he had seven hundred wives, princesses" (1 Kings 11:3). This indicates that most of his marriages were of a political nature. Probably the women came from small city-states and tribes surrounding Israel.

Village of Kafr Kenna. A village in rural Galilee, Kafr Kenna still looks much like the villages of biblical times. Notice the simple style of the houses.

After the Exodus, most Hebrew marriages were monogamous; each husband had only one wife (Mark 10:2-9). The Book of Proverbs never mentions polygamy, even though it touches on many aspects of Hebrew culture. The prophets always used the monogamous marriage to describe the Lord's relationship to Israel. Such a marriage was the ideal of family life.

C. Death of Husband. The death of a husband always has far-reaching consequences for his family. The people of biblical times were no exception. After a period of mourning, the widowed wife might follow several courses of action.

If she was childless, she was expected to continue living with her husband's family, according to the levirate law (Deut. 25:5-10). She was to marry one of her husband's brothers or a near kinsman. If these men were not available, she was free to marry outside the clan (Ruth 1:9).

Widows with children had other options open to them. From the deuterocanonical Book of Tobit we learn that some moved back to the family of their father or brother (Tobit 1:8). If the widow were elderly, one of her sons might care for her. If she had become financially secure, she might live alone. For example, Judith neither remarried nor moved into the home of a relative, for "her husband Manasses had left her gold, and silver, and men servants and maidservants, and cattle, and lands; and she remained upon this estate" (Judith 8:7).

Occasionally a widow was penniless and had no male relative to depend on. Such women faced great hardships (cf. 1 Kings 17:8-15; 2 Kings 4:1-7).

The childless widow of New Testament times found herself in a much more secure position. If she had no customary means of support, she could turn to the church for help. Paul suggests that young widows should remarry and that elderly widows should be cared for by their children; but if the widow could turn to no one, the church should care for her (1 Tim. 5:16).

D. Rebellious Children. It was a grave sin to dishonor one's father or mother. Moses ordered that a person who struck or cursed his parent should be put to death (cf. Exod. 21:15, 17; Lev. 20:9). We have no record of this punishment being given, but the Bible describes many instances in which children did dishonor their parents. When Ezekiel enumerated the sins of Jerusalem, he wrote, "In thee have they set light by father and mother; in the midst of thee have they dealt by oppression with the stranger: in thee have they vexed the fatherless and the widow" (Ezek. 22:7). A similar picture is presented in Proverbs 19:26. Jesus condemned many Jews of His day for not honoring their parents (Matt. 15:4-9).

Sometimes the parent caused more friction in a family than the child. The prophet Nathan announced to David that "the sword shall never depart from thine house, because thou hast despised me, and hast taken the wife of Uriah the Hittite to be thy wife" (2 Sam. 12:10). From that time on, David had problems with his sons.

Amnon fell passionately in love with Tamar, his half sister, and raped her. Yet David did not punish his son, and Tamar's brother Absalom killed Amnon in revenge. Then Absalom fled to his mother's country, returning later to lead a revolt against his father (2 Sam. 12). David urged his men not to kill Absalom, but the young man died in an accident of battle. David wept for him (2 Sam. 18).

As David neared his own death, his son Adonijah wanted to succeed him to the throne. David had not tried to restrain his wilfulness, in this or anything else. Scripture says that the king "had not displeased [Adonijah] at any time in saying, Why hast thou done so?" (1 Kings 1:6).

E. Sibling Rivalry. The writer of Proverbs graphically stated the problem of children who argue with one another: "A brother offended is harder to be won than a strong city: and their contentions are like the bars of a castle" (Prov. 18:19). The Bible describes brothers who quarreled for various reasons. Jacob sought to steal Esau's blessing for himself (Gen. 27). Absalom hated Amnon because David refused to punish him (2 Sam. 13). Solomon destroyed his brother Adonijah because he suspected that Adonijah wanted his throne (1 Kings 2:19-25). When Jehoram ascended the throne, he killed all his brothers so that they would never be a threat to him (2 Chron. 21:4).

Sometimes parents provoked sibling rivalry, as in the case of

Isaac's family. The Bible says that "Isaac loved Esau . . . , but Rebekah loved Jacob" (Gen. 25:28). When Isaac wanted to bless Esau, Rebekah helped Jacob get the blessing for himself. Esau became enraged and threatened to kill Jacob, who fled to a faraway country (Gen. 27:41-43). It took an entire generation to reunite their families.

Sadly, Jacob did not learn from his parents' mistakes. He also favored one of his sons, giving Joseph honor before the others. This so enraged the sons that they plotted to kill their father's favorite. Scripture records that "when his brethren saw that their father loved him more than all his brethren, they hated him, and could not speak peaceably unto him" (Gen. 37:4).

F. Adultery. The Hebrews considered adultery a serious threat to the family, so they punished adulterers swiftly and harshly.

SUMMARY

The family was a unifying thread of Bible history. When threatened or challenged, the family unit struggled for survival. God used families to convey his message to each new generation.

God has always expressed Himself as the Father of His redeemed family (Hos. 11:1-3). He expects honor from His children (Mal. 1:6). Jesus taught His disciples to pray, "Our Father." Even today, children's prayers prepare them to honor God as the perfect Father who is able to meet all their needs.

God ordained the family unit as a vital part of human society. Through the loving experience of a human family, we begin to understand the awesome privilege we have as a part of the "family of God."

2

WOMEN AND WOMANHOOD

It is fair to say that the people in biblical Israel felt that men were more important than women. The father or oldest male in the family made the decisions that affected the whole family, while the women had very little to say about them. This *patriarchal* (father-centered) form of family life set the tone for the way women were treated in Israel.

For example, a girl was raised to obey her father without question. Then when she married she was to obey her husband in the same way. If she were divorced, or widowed, she often returned to her father's house to live.

In fact, Leviticus 27:1-8 suggests that a woman was worth only half as much as a man. Thus a female child was less welcome than a male. Boys were taught to make decisions and to rule their families. Girls were raised to get married and have children.

A young woman didn't even think about a career outside the home. Her mother trained her to keep house and to raise children. She was expected to be a helper to her husband and to give him many children (Gen. 3:16). If a woman was childless, she was thought to be cursed (Gen. 30:1-2, 22; 1 Sam. 1:1-8).

Still, a woman was more than an object to be bought and sold. She had a very important role to play. Proverbs 12:4 says, "A virtuous woman is a crown to her husband, but she that maketh ashamed is as rottenness in his bones." In other words, a good wife was good for her husband; she helped him, looked after him and made him proud. But a bad wife was worse than a cancer; she could painfully destroy him and make him a mockery. A wife could make or break her husband.

Even though most women spent their days as housewives and mothers, there are some exceptions. For example, Miriam, Deborah, Huldah, and Esther were more than good wives—they were political and religious leaders who proved they could guide the nation as well as any man could.

GOD'S VIEW OF WOMEN

Toward the end of the first chapter of Genesis, we read: ". . . God created man in his own image, in the image of God created he him; male and female created he them. And God blessed them, and God said to them, Be fruitful, and multiply, and replenish the earth and subdue it: and have dominion over the fish of the sea, and over the fowl of the air, and over every living thing that moveth upon the earth" (Gen. 1:27-28). This passage shows two things about women. First, woman *as*

Portrait head. The black copper lines set into the eyelids of this ivory sculpture (fourteenth century B.C.) give a lifelike appearance to this representation of an important woman of Ugarit. Along the forehead at the hairline are loops of silver mixed with gold. The high headdress and the hair were once covered with thin gold.

well as man was created in the image of God. God did not create woman to be inferior to man; both are equally important. Second, the woman was also expected to have authority over God's creation. Man and woman are to share this authority—it does not belong only to the man.

God said, "It is not good that the man should be alone; I will make him a helper fit for him" (Gen. 2:18, RSV). So God "caused a deep sleep to fall upon Adam, and he slept: and he took one of his ribs" (Gen. 2:21). God used that rib in the creation of Eve. This account shows how important the woman is to a man: She is part of his very being, and without her man is incomplete.

But Adam and Eve sinned, and God told Eve, "Thy desire shall be to thy husband, and he shall rule over thee" (Gen. 3:16). So women were told to obey their husbands. That's the way it remained, even into New Testament times when the Apostle Paul told Christian wives, "submit yourselves unto your own husbands, as unto the Lord" (Eph. 5:22). But even though a woman was to obey her husband, she was not inferior to him. It just means that she should be willing to let him lead. In fact, Paul called for submission on the part of both the husband and the wife, "submitting yourselves one to another in the fear of God" (Eph. 5:21). In another letter, Paul clearly stated that there is no difference of status in Christ between a man and a woman. "There is neither Jew nor Greek," he writes, "there is neither bond nor free, there is neither male nor female: for ye are all one in Christ Jesus" (Gal. 3:28).

THE LEGAL POSITION OF WOMEN

The legal position of a woman in Israel was weaker than that of a man. For example, a husband could divorce his wife if he "found some uncleanness in her," but the wife was not allowed to divorce her husband for any reason (Deut. 24:1-4). The Law stated that a wife who was suspected of having sexual relations with another man must take a jealousy test (Num.

5:11-31). However, there was no test for a man suspected of being unfaithful with another woman. The Law also said that a man could make a religious vow and that it was binding on him (Num. 30:1-15); but a vow made by a woman could be cancelled by her father or (if she were married) by her husband. A woman's father could sell her to pay a debt (Exod. 21:7), and she could not be freed after 6 years, as a man could (Lev. 25:40). In at least one instance, a man gave his daughter to be used sexually by a mob (Judg. 19:24).

But some laws suggested that men and women were to be treated as equals. For example, children were to treat both parents with equal respect and reverence (Exod. 20:12). A son who disobeyed or cursed either parent was to be punished (Deut. 21:18-21). And a man and a woman caught in the act of adultery must both die by stoning (Deut. 22:22). (It is interesting to note here that when the Pharisees dragged an adulteress to Jesus and wanted to stone her, they had already broken the law themselves by letting the man get away—John 8:3-11.)

Other Hebrew laws offered protection for women. If a man took a second wife, he was still bound by law to feed and clothe his first wife, and to continue to have sexual relations with her (Exod. 21:10). Even the foreign woman who was taken as a war bride had some rights; if her husband got tired of her, she was to be set free (Deut. 21:14). Any man found guilty of the crime of rape was to be stoned to death (Deut. 22:23-27).

Usually, only men owned property. But when parents had no sons, their daughters could receive the inheritance. They had to marry within the clan to retain the inheritance (Num. 27:8-11).

Since Israel was a male dominated society, women's rights were sometimes overlooked. Jesus told of a widow who had to pester a judge that would not take time to listen to her side of the case. Because he didn't want her to keep bothering him, the judge finally agreed to her wishes (Luke 18:1-8). As with many of Jesus' stories, this was something that could really have happened, and perhaps did.

In spite of this widows were given some special privileges too. For example, they were allowed to glean the fields after the harvest (Deut. 24:19-22) and share a portion of the third-year tithe with the Levite (Deut. 26:12). So in spite of their weaker legal status, women did enjoy some special rights in Jewish society.

WOMEN AT WORSHIP

Women were considered to be members of the "family of faith." As such, they could enter into most of the areas of worship.

The Law directed all men to appear before the Lord three times a year. Apparently the women went with them on some occasions (Deut. 29:10; Neh. 8:2; Joel 2:16), but they were not required to go. Perhaps women were not required to go because of their important duties as wives and mothers. For instance, Hannah went to Shiloh with her husband and asked the Lord for a son (1 Sam. 1:3-5). Later, when the child was born, she told her husband, "I will not go up until the child be weaned, and then I will bring him, that he may appear before the Lord, and there abide for ever" (vv. 21-22).

Woman from Mari. A clay statuette from the city of Mari, located along the Euphrates River in Mesopotamia (now Syria), depicts a woman singing. The statuette was made sometime before 2500 B.C.

As head of the family, the husband or father presented the sacrifices and offerings on behalf of the entire family (Lev. 1:2). But the wife might also be present. Women attended the Feast of Tabernacles (Deut. 16:14), the yearly Feast of the Lord (Judg. 21:19-21), and the Festival of the New Moon (2 Kings 5:23).

One sacrifice that only the women gave to the Lord was offered after the birth of a child: "And when the days of her purifying are fulfilled, for a son, or for a daughter, she shall bring a lamb of the first year for a burnt offering, and a young pigeon, or a turtledove for a sin offering, unto the door of the tabernacle of the congregation, unto the priest" (Lev. 12:6).

Watershaft and steps. Built in about 1100 B.C., this stairway of seventy-nine steps spirals down to the pool of Gibeon. The stairway and shaft, which required the removal of almost 3000 tons of limestone, provided access to fresh water from within the city walls. Women of Gibeon made the long descent and climb every day to provide water for their households.

By New Testament times, the Jewish women had stopped being active in temple or synagogue worship. Although there was a special area at the temple known as the "Court of Women," women were not allowed to go into the inner court. Extra-biblical sources tell us that women were not allowed to read or to speak in the synagogue; but they could sit and listen in the special women's section. The women may have been allowed to enter only the synagogues that were operating on Hellenistic principles.

A different picture unfolds in the early Christian church. Luke 8:1-3 indicates that Jesus welcomed some women as traveling companions. He encouraged Martha and Mary to sit at His feet as disciples (Luke 10:38-42). Jesus' respect for women was something strikingly new.

After Jesus ascended into heaven, several women met with the other disciples in the Upper Room to pray. Even though Scripture does not say so specifically, these women probably prayed audibly in public. Both men and women gathered at the home of John Mark's mother to pray for the release of Peter (Acts 12:1-17), and both men and women prayed regularly in the church at Corinth (1 Cor. 11:2-16). That's why the apostle Paul gave instructions to both men and women about how to pray in public.

This freedom for women was so new that it caused some problems within the church, so Paul gave the early congregations some guidelines that limited the role of women. He wrote, "Let your women keep silence in the churches: for it is not permitted unto them to speak, but they are commanded to be under obedience, as also saith the law. And if they will learn any thing, let them ask their husbands at home: for it is a shame for women to speak in the church" (1 Cor. 14:34-35).

In another letter, Paul wrote, "Let the women learn in silence with all subjection. But I suffer not a woman to teach, nor to usurp authority over the man; but to be in silence" (1 Tim. 2:11-12). Opinions differ as to just what prompted Paul to write these things, and how far they constitute a rule for Christians today. Certainly, however, he was correcting behavior that appeared disorderly in his day.

Several Bible women were famous for their faith. Included in the list of faithful people in Hebrews 11 are two women, Sarah and Rahab (Josh. 2; 6:22-25). Hannah was a godly example of the Israelite mother: She prayed to God; she believed that God heard her prayers; and she kept her promise to God. Her story is found in 1 Samuel 1. Jesus' mother Mary was also a good and godly woman. In fact, Mary must have remembered Hannah's example, for her song of praise to God (Luke 1:46-55) was very similar to Hannah's song (1 Sam. 2:1-10). The apostle Paul reminded Timothy of the goodness of his mother and grandmother (2 Tim. 1:5).

Not all Jewish women in Bible times were loyal to God, however. According to the book of Jewish writings known as the Talmud, some women were "addicted to witchcraft" (Joma 83b) and the occult. The Talmud also alleged that "the majority of women are inclined to witchcraft" (Sanhedrin 67a). Some rabbis believed this was why God told Moses, "Thou shalt not suffer a witch to live." (Some translations render the Hebrew word for witch as *sorceress.)*

But to be fair, the Scriptures do not indicate that women were any more interested in the occult than the men were. Several scriptural references to women who were involved in the occult (e.g., 2 Kings 23:7; Ezek. 8:14; Hosea 4:13-14) clearly imply that men were also involved. And of the 4 times that sorcery is mentioned in the Book of Acts, only once was a woman involved (Acts 8:9-24; 13:4-12; 16:16-18; 19:13-16).

WOMEN IN ISRAEL'S CULTURE

Israelite society assumed that a woman's place was in the home. She was expected to find life most enjoyable as a wife and mother. Apparently Jewish women accepted that role willingly.

A. The Ideal Wife. Every man wanted to find a perfect wife, one who would do him "good and not evil, all the days of her life" (Prov. 31:12). Few men, then as now, wanted a wife who was bossy or who liked to fight! Proverbs 19:13 compared

Roman market scene. This Roman funerary relief shows the booth of a dealer in poultry and vegetables. A woman vendor stands behind the counter. The lot of Roman women was better than that of most women in the ancient world.

a wife's quarreling to the continual drip of rain on a person's head. In fact, "it is better to dwell in the wilderness, than with a contentious and an angry woman" (Prov. 21:19).

What qualities went into making the "perfect wife" in ancient Israel? What qualities did the family look for in a bride for their son? What qualities did a mother try to instill in her daughter to prepare her for being a good wife and mother?

Most of these qualities are described in an interesting poem in Proverbs 31. The poem is an *acrostic*—In other words, each verse begins with a different Hebrew letter in alphabetical order. We might call these verses the "ABC's of a Perfect Wife."

According to this poem, the ideal wife has many talents. She knows how to cook and to sew (vv. 13, 15, 19, 22). She never wastes her time with gossip, but spends her time in more important tasks (v. 27). She has a knack for seeing what needs to be done and doing it. She has a good understanding of business, knowing how to buy and sell wisely (vv. 16, 24). However, she is not selfish. She helps the needy and gives advice to those who are less wise (v. 26). She also has a deep reverence for God (v. 30). She tries in every way to be a "helper fit" for her husband. The poem ends by saying that if she does all these things, her husband will be lifted to an important place in the eyes of the community (v. 23).

A shorter outline of what makes a perfect wife can be found in Ecclesiasticus 26:13-16: "The grace of a wife delighteth her husband, and her discretion will fatten his bones. A silent and loving woman is a gift of the Lord; and there is nothing worth so much as a mind well instructed. A shamefaced [modest] and faithful woman is a double grace, and her continent mind cannot be valued. As the sun when it ariseth in the high heaven, so is the beauty of a good wife in the ordering of her house."

B. A Woman's Beauty. Each society has its own standards of beauty. Some cultures stress that a beautiful woman must be fat, while others applaud thinness. It is difficult to know just what the ancient Hebrews considered to be beautiful.

Most of the attractive women mentioned in the Bible are not described in detail. The writer usually notes that a woman was "beautiful," and that is all. The biblical concept of beauty is open to different interpretations.

Take, for example, the statement that "Leah's eyes were weak, but Rachel was beautiful and lovely" (Gen. 29:17, RSV). Some scholars think that the Hebrew word for "weak" could be better translated to mean "tender and charming" (cf. KJV, "tender-eyed"). If so, it might mean that each sister was beautiful in her own way. Leah might have had beautiful eyes, while Rachel had a beautiful body.

The clearest descriptions of a beautiful woman come from the Song of Solomon; but even here there is some doubt that the girl is being accurately described. The poet uses a long series of similes and metaphors to paint a mental picture of his love, and sometimes the poetic technique gets in the way of the description. Her teeth are white, like a flock of sheep, with none of them missing. Her lips are like a scarlet thread (Song of Sol. 4:2-3).

Some of the most important women in the Old Testament

were said to be beauties. Sarah (Gen. 12:11), Rebekah (Gen. 26:7), and Rachel (Gen. 29:17) are all described that way. David was tempted to commit adultery with Bath-sheba because she was so beautiful (2 Sam. 11:2). Tamar, David's daughter, was raped by her half-brother Amnon because of her beauty (2 Sam. 13:1). Both Absalom and Job had beautiful daughters (2 Sam. 14:27; Job 42:15). The struggle between Solomon and Adonijah to succeed David as king was ended when Adonijah asked to marry beautiful Abishag (1 Kings 1:3-4). Not only was his request denied, but it cost him his life

Hairdressing. A panel from the sarcophagus of Princess Kawit of Egypt (*ca.* 2100 B.C.) depicts the elaborate process of hairdressing. A servant braids her mistress' hair, while the princess holds a bowl of milk and a mirror.

(1 Kings 2:19-25). The Jews living during the Persian era were saved by a beautiful Jewess named Esther (cf. the Book of Esther).

Not all women were naturally beautiful, but the rich could improve their looks with expensive clothes, perfumes, and cosmetics. The prophet Ezekiel said that the nation of Israel was like a young woman who bathed and anointed herself. She wore fancy clothes and shoes made of leather. God said to the nation, "I decked thee also with ornaments, and I put bracelets upon thy hands and a chain on thy neck. And I put a jewel on thy forehead, and earrings in thine ears, and a beautiful crown upon thine head. Thus wast thou decked with gold and silver; and thy raiment was of fine linen and silk, and embroidered work" (Ezek. 16:11-13). The prophet Isaiah listed even more of this jewelry in Isaiah 3:18-23, such as anklets, headbands (KJV, "cauls"), amulets (KJV, "tablets"), signet rings, and nose rings. Some of these items have been found by archaeologists.

Jeremiah talked about another practice which was common in his day. Women painted lines on their faces to make their eyes more noticeable (Jer. 4:30). Other women put jeweled combs in their hair to make it look nicer. Many of these combs and hundreds of mirrors have also been found, dating all the way back to biblical times.

But there are two kinds of beauty—outer beauty and the inner beauty of a pleasing personality. The Scriptures warned men and women not to place too much importance on physical features and expensive clothes.

A wise man warned, "As a jewel of gold in a swine's snout, so is a fair woman which is without discretion" (Prov. 11:22). Another wise man wrote, "Favor is deceitful, and beauty is vain: but a woman that feareth the Lord, she shall be praised" (Prov. 31:30). Peter and Paul told the women of their day to be more concerned with inner beauty than with good looks (1 Tim. 2:9-10; 1 Pet. 3:3-4).

C. The Woman as Sexual Partner. It was against the Law for an unmarried woman to have sexual relations. She was to remain a virgin until after the marriage ceremony. If anyone could prove that she was *not* a virgin when she married, she was brought to the door of her father's house and the men of the city stoned her to death (Deut. 22:20-21).

But sex was a very important part of married life. God had ordained the sexual relationship to be enjoyed in the proper place and between the right people—marriage partners. The Jews felt so strongly about this that a newly married man was freed from his military or business duties for a whole year so that he could "cheer up his wife which he hath taken" (Deut. 24:5). The only restriction was that the husband and wife were not supposed to have sexual relations during her menstrual period (Lev. 18:19).

Sex was to be enjoyed by the wife as well as the husband. God told Eve, "Thy desire shall be to thy husband" (Gen. 3:16). In the Song of Solomon, the woman was very aggressive, kissing her husband and leading him into the bed chamber. She expressed her love for him over and over, and she urged him to enjoy their physical relationship (Song of Sol. 1:2; 2:3-6, 8-10; 8:1-4).

In New Testament times, there was a disagreement in the Corinthian church about the role of sex. Some people, it seems, felt that all of life was to be enjoyed, so whatever one wanted to do sexually should be all right—including adultery, prostitution, and homosexual acts. Other people thought that sex was somehow evil and that one should not have any physical relations at all, not even with one's husband or wife. Paul reminded the Corinthians that adultery and homosexuality were sins and should be avoided (1 Cor. 6:9-11). But he said husbands and wives should enjoy God's gift of sex together. Paul instructed that "the husband should give to the wife her conjugal rights, and likewise the wife to her husband. . . . Do not refuse one another except perhaps by agreement for a season, that you may devote yourselves to prayer; but then come together again, lest Satan tempt you through lack of self-control" (1 Cor. 7:3, 5, RSV).

D. The Woman as Mother. Without modern medicines and painkillers, childbirth was a very painful experience. In fact, many mothers died while giving birth (cf. Gen. 35:18-20;

1 Sam. 4:20). In spite of these dangers, most women still wanted to bear children.

Being a good wife and mother was extremely important to Hebrew women. The greatest honor a woman could have received would have been to give birth to the Messiah. We can hardly imagine Mary's excitement when the angel Gabriel greeted her with the words, "Hail, thou that art highly favored, the Lord is with thee! Blessed art thou among women!" (Luke 1:28). He then went on to tell her that she would be the Messiah's mother. The greeting that Mary received from Elizabeth was similar (cf. Luke 1:42).

E. A Woman's Work. By today's standards, we would not consider the daily life of the average Israelite mother to have been very stimulating. It was marked by hard work and long hours.

She was up each morning before anyone else, starting a fire in the hearth or oven. The main food in the Jewish diet was bread. In fact, the Hebrew word for food (*ohel*)was a synonym for bread. One of the jobs that the wife and mother had, then, was to grind grain into flour. This involved several steps. She had none of the electrical gadgets that modern wives have, so all of this work had to be done by hand.

She used thorns, stubble, or even animal dung to fuel the oven. The children usually had the job of finding the fuel; but

Kneading dough. This crudely modeled human figure from el-Jib in Palestine (*ca.* sixth century B.C.) bends over a trough to knead dough. Bread was the all-important staple food of the ancient Near East. Bakers mixed flour with water and seasoned it with salt, then kneaded it in the special trough. Then they added a small quantity of fermented dough until all the dough was leavened. The Jews did not use leaven in the offerings made by fire (Lev. 2:11), and its use was forbidden during Passover week.

if they were not old enough to leave the house, the woman had to find the fuel herself.

Every family needed water. Sometimes they built their own private cistern to store rain water; but most often the water came from a spring or well in the middle of the village. A few Old Testament cities were built above underground springs; Megiddo and Hazor were two of these cities. In Hazor a woman would walk through the streets to a deep shaft. Then she descended two manmade slopes for 9 m. (30 ft.) and five flights of stairs to the water tunnel, where she followed more stairs to the water level to fill her large water jug. She needed considerable strength to climb back out of the watershaft with a heavy water jug. But it wasn't all bad. The trip for water gave her a chance to talk with the other women of the village. The ladies would often gather around the water source in the evening or early morning to exchange news and gossip (cf. Gen. 24:11). The woman at the well at Sychar no doubt came at noon because the other women of the town didn't want anything to do with her because of her loose living and snubbed her when they met (cf. John 4:5-30).

The wife was also expected to make her family's clothes. Small children had to be nursed, watched, and kept clean. As the children got older, the mother taught them proper manners. She also taught the older daughters how to cook, sew, and do the other things a good Israelite wife must know about.

In addition, the wife was expected to help bring in the harvest (cf. Ruth 2:23). She prepared some crops like olives and grapes for storage. So her daily routine had to be flexible enough to include these other jobs.

WOMEN LEADERS IN ISRAEL

Most Israelite women never became public leaders, but there were some exceptions. Scripture records the names and deeds of several women who became prominent in political, military, or religious affairs.

A. Military Heroines. The two most famous military heroines in the Old Testament were Deborah and Jael; both had a part in the same victory. God spoke through Deborah to tell the general named Barak how the Canaanites could be beaten. Barak agreed to attack the Canaanites, but he wanted Deborah to go with him into the battle. She did so, and the Canaanites were duly defeated. However, the Canaanite general Sisera escaped on foot. Jael saw him, went out to greet him, and invited him into her tent. There he fell asleep. As he was sleeping, Jael came in and hammered a tent peg through his head, killing him (Judg. 4-5).

Another time several women helped defend their city of Thebez against attackers. The leader of the attack, Abimelech, moved in close to the tower gate to set it on fire. One of the women saw him at the gate and dropped a millstone on his head. The heavy stone crushed Abimelech's skull. As he lay

Women spinning wool. This stone relief from Susa depicts a woman holding a spindle in her left hand and a fibrous material, perhaps wool, in her right. Behind her stands a servant with a large fan. Among the Hebrews, spinning was mainly the occupation of women (Exod. 35:25-26).

dying he commanded his armor-bearer, "Draw thy sword and slay me, that men say not of me, A woman killed him" (Judg. 9:54). The attack was called off. Later generations gave the unidentified woman credit for the victory (cf. 2 Sam. 11:21).

A popular story told by the Jews in the days of Jesus was about a rich widow named Judith, who was devout and beautiful. The story began with Israel's being invaded by an Assyrian army, led by the general Holofernes. He surrounded one of the cities of Israel, cut off its food and supplies, and gave it 5 days to surrender. Judith encouraged her fellow townspeople to trust God for a victory. Then she put on beautiful clothes and paid a visit to Holofernes. The general thought she was very lovely and asked her to visit him every day. The last night before the Jews had to surrender, Judith was alone with Holofernes. When he fell into a drunken stupor, Judith took his sword, cut off his head, and put it in a basket. Then she returned to the city. In the morning, when the Assyrians found their leader was dead, the Jews won an easy victory.

B. Queens. Not all the women in the Bible were known for their good deeds. Queen Jezebel is the best-known evil woman in the Old Testament. She was a daughter of Ethbaal, king of the Sidonians. She married Ahab, the prince of Israel, and moved to Samaria. When Jezebel became queen, she forced her wishes on the people. She wanted the Israelites to bow down to Baal, so she brought hundreds of Baal's prophets into the country and put them on the government payroll. She also killed as many of the prophets of the Lord as she could find (1 Kings 18:13). Even godly laymen like Naboth were cut down. The prophet Elijah ran away and hid from Jezebel to save his life. He felt that he was the only true prophet left in the entire country. In fact, in the entire kingdom there were only 7,000 people who had refused to worship Baal, but only God knew who they were. Seven thousand, of course, was few enough. Years after Jezebel had been overthrown and killed, the worship of Baal continued (1 Kings 18–21).

Herodias was another woman who used her power and her beauty to get what she wanted. When John the Baptist spoke out against her marriage to King Herod, she got the king to arrest John and put him into prison. On Herod's birthday, Herodias' daughter danced for the guests. This pleased Herod very much, so he promised to give her anything she asked for. Herodias told her daughter to ask for the head of John the Baptist. In this way, she caused the death of John.

Not all the queens of the Bible were evil. Queen Esther used her power over the Persian Empire to help the Jews. A full account of her story can be found in the Book of Esther.

C. Queen Mothers. The writers of 1 and 2 Kings and 2 Chronicles tell us much about the queen mothers of Judah. In referring to the twenty different kings who ruled in Judah from the time of Solomon to the time of the Exile, only once do these books fail to mention a queen mother. A typical example of what is said about the queen mother is found in this passage: "In the second year of Joash the son of Joahaz king of Israel, Amaziah the son of Joash, king of Judah, began to reign. He was twenty-five years old when he began to reign, and he reigned twenty-nine years in Jerusalem. His mother's name was Jehoaddin of Jerusalem. And he did what was right in the eyes of the Lord" (2 Kings 14:1-3, RSV).

We assume that the mother of the king must have been an important person in Judah. Unfortunately, very little is known about her role in the government or the society.

One instance of a queen mother's having decisive influence may be noted. Because Adonijah was David's oldest surviving son, he felt he should be the next king after David. Several high officials agreed with him—including Joab, the general of the army, and Abiathar, the priest. On the other hand, the prophet Nathan and another priest named Zadok believed Solomon, another of David's sons, would be a better king. Bath-sheba, Solomon's mother, persuaded David to vow that Solomon would be king (1 Kings 1:30). Solomon respected his mother for what she had done (1 Kings 2:19).

Not all queen mothers were treated so respectfully, however. When King Asa brought religious reforms to the country, he removed his mother from her position at the court. She had made an image of the goddess Asherah. Because King Asa felt these things were sinful, he removed the prostitutes and destroyed all the idols, including the one of Asherah. While

Woman's head of ivory.
This ivory head of an
Assyrian woman (*ca.*
eighth century B.C.) was
carved from a section of a
large elephant's tusk. A
double-strand fillet or
headband holds the hair,
which falls in curls down
the neck.

King Asa did not kill his mother, he took away her power (1 Kings 15:9-15).

One queen mother who had tremendous power was Athaliah, the mother of Ahaziah. When her son was killed in battle, Athaliah seized the throne and tried to kill all the rightful heirs. But one of the infant princes was hidden from her. For 6 years Athaliah ruled Judah with an iron hand; but as soon as the young prince was old enough to become king, Athaliah was overthrown and killed (2 Kings 11:1-16).

D. Counselors. Most villages had wise persons whom other people often asked for advice. The king's court had many wise counselors as well. While there are no Scripture references to women counselors in the king's court, there are several examples of village wise women.

When Joab, the commander-in-chief of David's army, wanted to reconcile David and his son Absalom, he got a wise woman from Tekoa to help him. The woman pretended to be a widow with two sons. She said that one of her sons had killed the other in a fit of anger, and now the rest of her family wanted to kill the remaining son. David listened to her story

The Mezuzah

When the angel of death passed over Egypt, killing all first-born males, Jewish families were protected by the blood of the paschal lamb on the doorposts of their homes (Exod. 12:23). Today many Jews attach a *mezuzah* to their doorposts as a reminder of God's presence and the Jewish people's redemption from Egypt.

The *mezuzah* (Hebrew, "doorpost") is a small case containing a parchment on which the following prayer is written: "Hear, O Israel, the Lord our God, the Lord is One. And thou shalt love the Lord thy God with all thy heart, and with all thy soul, and with all thy might. And these words which I command thee this day shall be upon thy heart. Thou shalt teach them diligently unto thy children, and shalt speak of them when thou sittest in thy house, when thou walkest by the way, when thou liest down and when thou riseth up. And thou shalt bind them for a sign upon thy hand and they shall be for frontlets between thine eyes. And thou shalt write them upon the doorposts of thy house and upon thy gates" (Deut. 6:4-9).

The parchment continues with Deuteronomy 11:13-21, which emphasizes obedience to the commandments and the rewards of a righteous life.

Even today each mezuzah parchment is carefully written by qualified scribes, using the same strict procedures they use in writing the Laws. It is then tightly rolled and placed in its case so that the word *shaddai* ("Almighty") appears through a small hole near the top. A special prayer is read when the mezuzah is attached near the top of the right-hand doorpost. Though the popularity of the mezuzah has diminished in recent years, many Jews still kiss the mezuzah by touching their lips with their fingers and raising the fingers to a mezuzah when entering or leaving the home. At the same time, they recite Psalm 121:8. "The Lord shall preserve thy going out and thy coming in from this time forth, and even forevermore."

The mezuzah is a Jewish family's daily reminder of their responsibility to God and their community. It is a sign to the community that this home is one where the laws of God reign supreme. Within this sanctuary, away from wordly influences, the Jewish family studies the Scripture, observes religious holidays, and instructs their children in the faith of their fathers.

An ancient Hebrew scholar explained the purpose of the mezuzah by comparing it to the guards of an earthly king. In the same way that a king has guards at the gate to assure him of his security, the people of Israel are safe within their homes because the word of God is at the door to guard them.

and ruled that she was right to forgive this second son. Then the woman pointed out to the king that he was not practicing what he preached, for he had not forgiven Absalom for a similar crime. David saw that he had been wrong and allowed Absalom to return to Jerusalem (2 Sam. 14:1-20).

Another wise woman saved her town from destruction. A

man named Sheba led a revolt against King David. When the revolt failed, Sheba ran away and hid in the city of Abel. David's general Joab surrounded the city and was getting ready to attack it when a wise woman from the city appeared at the wall and asked to speak to Joab. She reminded him how important her town had been to Israel; she said that to destroy this city of Abel would be like killing "a mother in Israel." So together they agreed to a plan. If Sheba were killed, the city would not be attacked. The wise woman returned and told the townspeople about the plan. They killed Sheba and watched Joab and his army ride away.

E. Religious Leaders. In Israel, God did not prescribe priestesses, and a woman could not in any case have become a priest because her monthly cycle made her unclean. Priestly ministry was restricted to the male descendants of Aaron. However, women could perform many other ritual tasks. It is not surprising to find women involved in the public worship of God on various levels.

Women served as prophetesses—that is, spokeswomen for God. The most famous Hebrew prophetess was Huldah, the wife of Shallum. She was active in this ministry during the days of King Josiah. When the book of the Law was found in the temple, the religious leaders came to her and asked what God wanted the nation to do. The whole nation, including King Josiah, tried to carry out her instructions to the last detail, for they were sure God had spoken through her (2 Kings 22:11–23:14).

There were many other Old Testament prophetesses, including Miriam (Exod. 15:20), Deborah (Judg. 4:4), and Isaiah's wife (Isa. 8:3). The New Testament mentions that Anna and the daughters of Philip were prophetesses, but we don't know much else about their lives or their messages (Luke 2:36; Acts 21:9).

Some women used the musical talents God had given them. Miriam and other women sang a song of praise to God after the Israelites had been delivered from the Egyptians (Exod. 15:2). When God helped Deborah and Barak defeat the Canaanites, they wrote a victory song and sang it as a duet

(Judg. 5:1-31). Three daughters of Heman were also musicians; according to 1 Chronicles 25:5, they performed at the temple.

In the church at Cenchreae there was a deaconess named Phoebe, who Paul said was "a helper of many and of myself as well" (Rom. 16:2, RSV). In a letter to Timothy, Paul wrote that wives of deacons "must be serious, no slanderers, but temperate, faithful in all things" (1 Tim. 3:11, RSV). But he made it clear that he did not want any woman to teach or to have authority over men (2:12).

Other female leaders of the early church included Priscilla, who explained to Apollos "the way of God more perfectly" (cf. Acts 18:24-28). Euodias and Syntyche were two of the spiritual leaders at Philippi. Paul said, "They have labored side by side with me in the gospel together with Clement and the rest of my fellow workers" (Phil. 4:3, RSV). Thus it appears that they were doing a work which was similar to his own.

SUMMARY

An old Jewish story demonstrates how important the woman was in Israel. The story says that a pious man once married a pious woman. They were childless, so they eventually agreed to divorce one another. The husband then married a wicked woman and she made him wicked. The pious woman married a wicked man and made him righteous. The moral of the story is that the woman set the tone for the home.

The Israelite mother held an important place in the life of the family. To a large degree, she was the key to a successful family or the cause of its failure. She could have incalculable influence on her husband and her children.

Israel's history and its culture owes a great deal to these hard-working women.

3

MARRIAGE AND DIVORCE

The Bible clearly expresses God's intentions for marriage. In marriage, a man and a woman are meant to find fulfillment that is both spiritual and sexual. This relationship was marred by mankind's fall into sin. The history of Israel tells of changes that affected marriage because the Israelites chose to accept the degrading practices of their ungodly neighbors.

Jesus reaffirmed what marriage means. He rebuked the Jews' attitude toward divorce, and he challenged marriage partners to live in harmony with one another.

MARRIAGE

We should notice these Bible passages that describe the purpose of marriage. Scripture gives a full-orbed view of the privileges and duties of the marriage bond.

A. Divinely Established. God first created a pair of human beings, a man and a woman. His first command to them was, "Be fruitful, and multiply, and replenish the earth" (Gen. 1:28). By putting this couple together, God instituted marriage, the most basic of all social relationships. Marriage enabled mankind to fulfill God's command to rule and replenish the earth (Gen. 1:28).

God made both the male and the female in His image, each with a special role and each complemented by the other. Genesis 2 tells us that God created the man first. Then, using a rib from the man, God made a "help meet for him" (Gen. 2:18). When God brought Eve to Adam, He joined them together and said, "Therefore shall a man leave his father and his mother, and shall cleave unto his wife: and they shall be one flesh" (Gen. 2:24).

God intended marriage to be a permanent relationship. It was to be a unique covenantal commitment of two people that excluded all others from its intimacy. God expressly forbade the breaking of that union when He gave the commandment, "Thou shalt not commit adultery" (Exod. 20:14). The New Testament reaffirms the uniqueness of the marriage bond. Jesus said that a man and his wife "are no more twain, but one flesh. What therefore God hath joined together, let not man put asunder" (Matt. 19:6). Paul beautifully compared the love of a man for his wife to the love of Christ for His church (Eph. 5:25). He said that Christ's love was so deep that He died for the church, and in the same way a man's love for his wife should overcome any sense of the imperfections she may have.

Marriage is more than a contract that two people make for

Wedding procession.
This artist's conception of a typical wedding procession in biblical times shows a bridegroom escorting the wedding party back to his house for a feast. Music and dancing were major parts of the celebration, which lasted for one to two weeks.

their mutual benefit. Because they make their marriage vows in God's presence and in His name, they may draw power from God to fulfill those vows. God becomes a supporting party to the marriage. Proverbs reminds us of this when it says that God gives wisdom, discretion, and understanding so that marriage partners can avoid being lured into unfaithfulness (cf. Prov. 2:6-16). New Testament writers understood that Christian marriage is created and maintained by Christ.

B. Marked by Love. Above all else, love is to mark the union. Note the simplicity with which Scripture describes the marriage of Isaac and Rebekah: "[He] took Rebekah, and she became his wife; and he loved her" (Gen. 24:67). Love, based on true friendship and respect, seals and sustains the marriage bond. Peter calls husbands to "dwell with them [your wives] according to knowledge, giving honor unto the wife, as unto the weaker vessel, and as being heirs together of the grace of life" (1 Pet. 3:7). When this kind of love exists between a man and wife, it purifies their marriage relationship.

The Bible says that husband and wife are equal as persons before God, since both have been made in God's image. Both can be saved from their sins through Jesus (Gen. 1:28; Gal. 3:28; Col. 3:10-11). Together they receive God's gifts and blessings for their marriage (Rom. 4:18-21; Heb. 11:11; 1 Pet. 3:5-7). When they join in marriage, they both have the obligations, though they may have varying degrees of ability to perform the responsibilities they share.

C. Sexually Fulfilling. Another factor in the marriage relationship is the sexual union of the partners. Sexual union consummates marriage on the basis of a mutual matrimonial commitment. The expression, "he knew his wife" (Gen. 4:1, 25, and other places), is the Bible's straightforward way of referring to sexual intercourse. But the Bible treats this act with dignity, calling it honorable and undefiled (Heb. 13:4). Scripture calls on God's people to keep their sexual relations pure. They are not to use sex to fulfill lustful passions, as the ungodly do (1 Thess. 4:3-7). Scripture encourages a married man to delight in the wife of his youth all his life (Eccles. 9:9). He is to be "ravished always with her love" (Prov. 5:15-19).

1. A Duty to Consummate. When a man of Israel became engaged to marry, he was not to let anything keep him from fulfilling his purpose. He was not to go to war, lest he die and another man marry his promised bride (Deut. 20:7). For the first year of marriage, he was not to resume any task that would interfere with his presence at home to "cheer up his wife" (Deut. 24:5). Paul told husbands and wives to be sexually available to each other, without depriving one another, so that

Wedding scenes. Scenes from a typical Roman wedding are shown on the sides of this altar. In the scene at left, the couple joins hands at the conclusion of the marriage service. At right, children take part in the procession to the bridegroom's house, carrying an offering for pagan sacrifice.

Satan would not be able to tempt them to indulge roving affections because they lacked self-control (1 Cor. 7:3-5).

2. Promiscuity and Perversion. Paul says that a man who joins himself "to a harlot is one body [with her], for two [the man and the harlot] . . . shall be one flesh" (1 Cor. 6:16). The body, Paul says, is the temple of Christ. Since a promiscuous sexual union joins the flesh of two individuals, it is a defilement of Christ's holy place.

Here the term *flesh* means more than the sexual organs or even the entire body. It refers to the whole person. Sexual union inescapably involves the whole person, whether within or outside marriage. When God demands that His people live holy lives (1 Pet. 1:15-16), this includes their sexual conduct in relation to their marriage (1 Thess. 4:3-6). He required corresponding holiness of the Israelites (Lev. 18; 20:10-21). The whole person—body no less than soul—is set apart for God.

The cult prostitution of pagan nations eventually found its way into Israel. The very presence of this practice profaned the worship of the Lord (1 Sam. 2:22).

The Bible forbids incest (Lev. 18:6-18; 20:11-12). Also, it denounces homosexual relations as being perverse and despicable in God's eyes. In fact, such relations carried a death penalty in Israel (cf. Lev. 18:22; 20:13; Deut. 23:18; Rom. 1:26-27; 1 Cor. 6:9; 1 Tim. 1:10).

3. Proper Sexual Roles. In biblical times, marriage was thought of as a state in which persons would naturally fulfill their respective sexual roles. Thus the man was head of his family and the wife was to submit to his authority (Psa. 45:11; 1 Pet. 3:4-6). This role relationship was present at the very beginning; the woman was made to be the man's helper, suited to him in that sense. Throughout the time of the Old Testament, the woman found her place in society through her father, then through her husband, and then through her older brother or kinsman-redeemer. God worked through this role relationship to establish harmony in the family and in the whole of society.

The submission of a Jewish woman to her husband did not depreciate her abilities or demote her to a secondary place in society. The "excellent" wife of the Old Testament (Prov. 31) enjoyed the confidence of her husband and the respect of her children and neighbors. She had a great deal of freedom to use her economic skills to provide for her family. She was recognized as a person of wisdom and a gracious teacher. She was as far as possible from being a chattel slave, which is how a woman was regarded in other Near Eastern cultures.

D. A Spiritual Symbol. Marriage symbolized the union between God and His people. Israel was called the Lord's wife, and the Lord Himself said, "I was a husband unto them" (Jer. 31:32; cf. Isa. 54:5). Prophets declared that the nation had committed "fornication" and "adultery" when it turned from God to idols (Num. 25:1; Judg. 2:17; Jer. 3:20; Ezek. 16:17; Hos. 1:2). They said that God had divorced His "unfaithful wife" (Isa. 50:1; Jer. 3:8) when He sent the Israelites away into captivity. Yet God had compassion on His "wife," Israel, and called "her" back to be faithful (Isa. 54). As a bridegroom delights in his bride (Isa. 62:4-5), so the Lord delighted to make Israel the "holy people," His redeemed ones (Isa. 62:12).

The New Testament describes the church as the bride of Christ, preparing herself for life in the eternal kingdom (Eph. 5:23). This image underlines the truth that marriage ought to be an exclusive and permanent union of love and fidelity. Husbands should love their wives as Christ loves His ransomed bride, and wives should submit to their husbands, as they submit to Christ.

BIBLICAL MARRIAGE CUSTOMS

In biblical times, the first step in marriage was taken by the man or his family (Gen. 4:19; 6:2; 12:19; 24:67; Exod. 2:1). Usually the couples' families made the marriage arrangement. Thus Hagar, as head of the family, "took him [Ishmael] a wife out of the land of Egypt" (Gen. 21:21). When Isaac was forty years old, he was quite capable of choosing his own wife (Gen. 25:20); yet Abraham sent his servant to Haran to seek a wife for Isaac (Gen. 24).

Abraham gave his servant two strict orders: The bride must not be a Canaanite, and she must leave her home to live with Isaac in the Promised Land. Under no circumstance was Isaac to return to Haran to live according to their former way of life.

Abraham's servant found the Lord's direction in his choice (Gen. 24:12-32). Then, according to Mesopotamian custom, he made arrangements with the girl's brother and mother (Gen. 24:28-29, 33). He sealed the agreement by giving gifts (a dowry) to them and to Rebekah (Gen. 24:53). Finally, they sought Rebekah's own consent (Gen. 24:57). This procedure was very similar to Hurrian marriage practices described in ancient texts from Nuzi. [1]

Under different circumstances, both of Isaac's sons—Jacob and Esau—chose their own wives. Esau's choice caused much distress to his parents (Gen. 26:34-35; 27:46; 28:8-9); but Jacob's choice met with approval.

Jacob was sent to Laban, his uncle in Haran, where he acted on his father's authority to arrange to marry Rachel. Instead of giving Laban a dowry, he worked for 7 years. But it was not customary to allow the younger daughter to marry first, so Laban tricked Jacob into marrying Rachel's older sister, Leah. Jacob then accepted Laban's offer to work 7 more years for Rachel.

In that region, a man who had no sons often adopted a male heir, giving him his daughter as wife. The adopted son was required to labor in the household. If a natural son was born later, the adopted son lost his inheritance to the natural heir. Laban may have intended to adopt Jacob; but then sons were born to him (Gen. 31:1). Perhaps Laban's sons grew jealous of Jacob because they feared he might claim the inheritance. At any rate, Jacob left Haran secretly to return to his father in Canaan.

Rachel took along the household gods of her father. Since the possession of these gods was a claim to inheritance, Laban followed in hot pursuit; but Rachel concealed the idols so that Laban did not find them. To pacify his uncle, Jacob pledged not to mistreat Laban's daughters or take other wives (Gen. 31:50).

We should especially note the Old Testament tradition of the "bride price." As we have seen, the husband or his family paid a bride price to the father of the bride to seal the marriage agreement (cf. Exod. 22:16-17; Deut. 22:28-29).

The bride price was not always paid in cash. It might be given in the form of clothing (Judg. 14:8-20) or some other valuable item. A most gruesome one was demanded by Saul, who asked David for physical proof that he had killed 100 Philistines (1 Sam. 18:25).

The giving of a bride price did not indicate that the wife had been sold to the husband and was his property. It was a realization of the economic worth of the daughter. Later the law recognized the practice of buying a female servant to become a man's wife. Such laws protected women from abuse or maltreatment (Exod. 21:7-11).

At times, the groom or his family gave gifts to the bride too (Gen. 24:53). Sometimes the bride's father also gave her a wedding gift, as Caleb did (Josh. 15:15-19). In this connection, it is interesting to note that the Egyptian pharaoh gave the city of Gezer as a wedding gift to his daughter, Solomon's wife (1 Kings 9:16).

The feast was an important part of the marriage ceremony. It was usually given by the bride's family (Gen. 29:22), but the groom's family might give it too (Judg. 14:10).

Both the bride and the groom had attendants to serve them (Judg. 14:11; Psa. 45:14; Mark 2:19). If it were a royal wedding, the bride gave her attendants to her husband to add to the glory of his court (Psa. 45:14).

Even though the bride would adorn herself with jewels and beautiful clothing (Psa. 45:13-15; Isa. 49:18), the groom was the center of attention. The Psalmist focuses, not on the bride (as modern Westerners might do), but on the bridegroom as being happy and radiant on the wedding day (Psa. 19:5).

In other Near Eastern nations, the groom customarily went to live with the bride's family. But in Israel, the bride usually went to her husband's home and became part of his family. The right of inheritance followed the male. If an Israelite had only daughters and wanted to preserve his family inheritance, his daughters had to marry within their tribe because the inheritance could not be transferred to another tribe (Num. 36:5-9).

One of the most important aspects of the marriage celebration was the pronouncement of God's blessing upon the union. This is why Isaac blessed Jacob before sending him to Haran to seek a wife (Gen. 24:60; 28:1-4).

Although Scripture does not describe a marriage ceremony, we assume that it was a very public event. Jesus attended and blessed at least one marriage ceremony. He referred to various aspects of the wedding festivities in His lessons, thus showing that marriage ceremonies were familiar to the common person (Matt. 22:1-10; 25:1-3; Mark 2:19-20; Luke 14:8).

Both families were involved in planning the marriage. The bride's family also assumed responsibility for keeping evidence that she was a virgin on the wedding day, in case her husband later maligned her (Deut. 22:13-19).

LEVIRATE MARRIAGE

The Israelites felt that it was very important for a man to have an heir. To preserve the property inheritance that God had given them, they had to convey it through family lines (cf. Exod. 15:17-18; Psa. 127:128).

A woman who was unable to have children often felt the rebuke of her neighbor (Gen. 30:1-2, 23; 1 Sam. 1:6-10; Luke 1:25). She and her family would then retreat into earnest prayer (Gen. 25:21; 1 Sam. 1:10-12, 26-28).

A more serious situation arose if her husband died before she had borne an heir. To solve this problem, the practice of *levirate marriage* was begun. First mentioned in connection with the family of Judah (Gen. 38:8), levirate marriage later became a part of the Law of Moses (Deut. 25:5-10). When a woman was widowed, her dead husband's brother would marry her according to levirate law. The children of this marriage because the heirs of the deceased brother, in order that "his name be not put out of Israel" (Deut. 25:6). If a man refused to marry his widowed sister-in-law, he was publicly disgraced (Deut. 25:7-10; cf. Ruth 4:1-7).

The most familiar example of this was the marriage of Boaz to Ruth. In this case, the nearest of kin was unwilling to marry Ruth; so Boaz, as the next-nearest of kin, acted as the kinsman-redeemer. Having paid the indebtedness on Elimelech's inheritance, he took Ruth to be his wife "to raise up the name of the dead upon his inheritance, that the name of the dead be not cut off from among his brethren, and from the gate of his place" (Ruth 4:10). David was the third generation from this marriage, and from this line later came Jesus Christ (Ruth 4:17; Rom. 1:3).

VIOLATIONS OF MARRIAGE

Although God ordained marriage as a holy relationship between one man and one woman, it soon was corrupted when some men took two wives (cf. Gen. 4:19). Intermarriage with foreign people and the adoption of pagan ways compounded the problem.

Scripture records that Abraham followed the heathen custom of begetting a child to be his heir by a slave girl, because his wife was barren. "I pray thee go in unto my maid," Sarah asked her husband. "It may be that I may obtain children by her" (Gen. 16:2). The slave girl, Hagar, soon bore a son for Abraham. Later, Sarah also gave birth to a son. Hagar's arrogance vexed Sarah and caused her to treat Hagar harshly. When Sarah observed Ishmael making fun of her own son, she decided she had endured enough. She demanded that Abraham send Hagar away. Because Hagar had borne him a son, Abraham could not sell her as a slave. He gave Hagar her freedom and sent her away with a gift (Gen. 21:14; 25:6).

Jacob was another Hebrew patriarch who followed pagan marriage customs. Jacob took two wives because his uncle had tricked him into marrying the wrong woman (Gen. 29:21-30). When Rachel realized that she was barren, she gave Jacob her maid "that I may also have children" (Gen. 30:3-6). Leah became jealous and gave Jacob her own servant to bear more children in her name (Gen. 30:9-13). Thus Jacob had two wives and two concubines, but he gave equal status to all his children as heirs of the covenant (Gen. 46:8-27; 49).

Beginning with David, the kings of Israel indulged themselves with the luxury of many wives and concubines, even though God had specifically commanded them not to do this (Deut. 17:17). This practice gave them social status and enabled them to make various political alliances (2 Sam. 3:2-5; 5:13-16; 12:7-10; 1 Kings 3:1; 11:1-4).

David fell into adultery with Bath-sheba and eventually committed murder in order to marry her. Death was the customary punishment for this sin (Lev. 20:10; Deut. 22:22). But instead of taking David's life, God decreed that the child of David and Bath-sheba should die, and that strife should rise up against David in his own household (2 Sam. 12:1-23).

Solomon also was punished for disobeying God's commands concerning marriage. His many foreign wives led him into idolatry (1 Kings 11:4-5).

The Mosaic Law gave protection to concubines and multiple wives, but not in order to sanction the practice. The law gave secondary status to concubines and their children to protect these innocent victims of uncontrolled lust (Exod. 21:7-11; Deut. 21:10-17). We should view the law's allowance of these practices in the light of Jesus' comment on divorce: "Moses, because of the hardness of your hearts, suffered you to put away your wives; but from the beginning it was not so" (Matt. 19:8).

Malachi spoke out against the abuse and neglect that a wife suffered when her husband turned to pagan women and divorced her. The marriage covenant called her to bear "godly seed"; but the man's unfaithfulness led him to ignore his responsibilities to her (Mal. 2:11, 14-16).

Mosaic Law did not allow Israelites to marry foreign women (Deut. 7:3) because they worshiped other gods. When the Israelites returned from captivity, they were reminded that marrying foreign wives was contrary to God's Law. Ezra and Nehemiah spoke on the matter many times (Ezra 10; Neh.

10:30; 13:23-28). Nehemiah rebuked his generation by saying, "Did not Solomon king of Israel sin by these things? . . . Even him did outlandish women cause him to sin" (Neh. 13:26; cf. 1 Kings 11:4-5). Ezra required every man to end his relationship with his foreign wife. Those who refused were banned from the congregation and their property was seized (Ezra 10:8).

The sexual relationship that God intended was *monogamy*— one man and one woman. But because of degraded human passions, God's Law needed to prohibit specific sexual sins (Lev. 18:1-30; 20:10-24; Deut. 27:20-23).

Even so, some men went to harlots unashamedly (Gen. 38:15-23; Judg. 16:11). The Book of Proverbs warned at length against loose and evil women who solicited young men

Royal couple. This painted limestone relief from about 1370 B.C. depicts an Egyptian queen offering flowers to the king, who casually leans on his staff. This and other inscriptions show that the queen played a secondary role in the royal family.

in the streets (Prov. 2:16-19; 5:1-23; 6:20-35). Canaanite cult prostitution was a grave abuse, which was occasionally practiced in Israel (1 Sam. 2:22-25; 1 Kings 15:12; 2 Kings 23:7; Hos. 4:13-14; cf, Deut. 23:17).

Several biblical lists of sins began with sexual immorality (Mark 7:21; Rom. 1:24-27; 1 Cor. 6:9; Gal. 5:19; Eph. 5:5). Any sexual sin mocked the image of God in man. God warned that He would destroy any society that allowed such sin to continue (Lev. 18:24-29).

THE SINGLE PERSON

By His words and by His own unmarried life, Jesus showed that marriage was not an end in itself, nor was it essential to the wholeness of a person. As God's servant, a person might not be called to have a mate and children. A Christian disciple might need to forget parents and possessions for the sake of the kingdom of God (Luke 18:29; cf. Matt. 19:29; Mark 10:29-30).

Paul wished that all men could be content to live unmarried like him (1 Cor. 7:7-8). He found full freedom and completeness in attending "upon the Lord without distraction" (1 Cor. 7:35). But he recognized that a person who does not have the gift of self-control in this area should marry, so that "he sinneth not" (1 Cor. 7:9, 36).

DIVORCE

Bible scholars disagree over the way Jesus and Paul interpreted the Mosaic Law concerning divorce. Yet the provisions of the Old Testament are quite clear.

A. Mosaic Law. The Law of Moses allowed a man to divorce his wife when she found "no favor in his eyes, because he hath found some uncleanness in her" (Deut. 24:1). The primary thrust of this piece of legislation was to prevent him from taking her again after she had married another man;

this would have been an "abomination before the Lord" (Deut. 24:4).

The Law was supposed to deter divorce rather than encourage it. It required a "writing of divorcement"—a public document granting the woman the right to remarry without civil or religious sanction. Divorce could not be done privately.

The acceptable reason for granting divorce was "some uncleanness." Specific types of "uncleanness" had their own penalties. For example, adultery carried the death penalty by stoning.

If a man believed his wife was not a virgin when he married her, he could take her to the elders of the city. If they judged her guilty, her punishment was death (Deut. 22:13-21). However, if the man had falsely accused his wife, he would be chastised and required to pay her father twice the usual bride price.

When the husband suspected his wife of adultery, he took her to the priest, who gave her the "jealousy test." This was a "trial by ordeal" typical of ancient Near Eastern cultures. The woman was made to drink bitter water. If she were innocent, then the water did not affect her. If she were guilty, she would become ill. In that case, she was stoned to death as an adulteress (Num. 5:11-31).

Although the Law of Moses allowed a man to divorce his wife, the wife was not allowed to divorce her husband for any reason at all. Many women probably fled from unpleasant circumstances without a bill of divorcement (cf. Judg. 19:2). Legally the wife was bound to her husband as long as they both lived or until he divorced her. If the woman was given a certificate of divorce, she was eligible to remarry any man except a priest (Lev. 21:7, 14; Ezek. 44:22).

However, remarriage defiled her in respect to her first husband—i.e., he could not marry her again, because she had in effect committed adultery against him (cf. Matt. 5:32).

Despite the provisions allowing divorce, God did not approve of it. "He hateth putting away"; He called it "violence" and "dealing treacherously" (Mal. 2:16).

B. Jesus' Teachings. In Jesus' day, there was much confu-

Divorce in Babylon

Marriage is an ancient ritual; so is divorce. Perhaps there is nothing so basic to a culture as its rules concerning the relationship of man and woman.

Hammurabi, a Babylonian king who ruled from 1728 to 1686 B.C. constructed intricate laws called the Code of Hammurabi. These laws dealt with all aspects of Babylonian life, including divorce. Hammurabi's divorce laws were almost as complicated as divorce law today.

A Babylonian husband could simply say to his wife, "Thou art not my wife" *(ul assati atti)*, or that he "had left" or "divorced" her. He gave her "leaving money" or "divorce money." It was also sometimes said that he "had cut the fringe of her garment." Since a garment often symbolized the person who wore it, this meant that the husband had cut his marriage tie to his wife. His words were a legal divorce decree.

The Babylonian wife might say that "she has hated" her husband or that she "has left him," which meant that she refused to have sexual relations with him. However, nothing the woman said could dissolve the marriage. She did not have the power to divorce her husband without a court's consent.

Divorce was not an issue unless the marriage had been formalized. "If a man acquire a wife, but did not draw up the contracts for her, that woman is no wife," according to the Hammurabi Code. Once people were legally married, however, the conditions and consequences of divorce were clearly outlined in the Code. There were divorce laws concerning unconsummated marriages, childless marriages, marriage to a priestess, marriage in which the husband was taken captive during a war, marriage in which the wife became seriously ill; and always there were specific provisions about who was to receive what sum of money.

A husband could divorce his wife almost at will. However, if she was not at fault, the man had to give up her dowry, often a large portion of his property. This protected the wife from capricious or casual divorce. If there was misconduct by husband or wife, the courts were expected to assess punishment. A woman could never start divorce proceedings; she had to wait for her husband to apply to the court. If a woman could not prove her own innocence *and* her husband's guilt, she was drowned. Needless to say, only in extreme cases did a woman seek divorce. If the husband was found to be at fault, the wife "incurs no punishment" for her refusal of conjugal rights and could return to her father's house.

A woman could even be divorced if she was "a gadabout, thus neglecting her "house and humiliating her husband." If found guilty of this crime, "they shall throw that woman into the water."

Nothing was sacred or perpetual about marriage in Babylonia. It seems to have been a secular agreement rather than a religious or moral commitment.

sion about the grounds for divorce. The rabbis could not agree on what constituted the "uncleanness" of Deuteronomy 24:1. There were two opinions. Those following Rabbi Shammai felt adultery was the only grounds for divorce. Those who followed Rabbi Hillel accepted a number of reasons for divorce, including such things as poor cooking.

The Gospels record four statements by Jesus concerning divorce. In two of these, He allowed divorce in the case of adultery.

In Matthew 5:32, Jesus commented on the position of both

the woman and her new husband: "Whosoever shall put away his wife, saving for the cause of fornication, causeth her to commit adultery: and whosoever shall marry her that is divorced committeth adultery." In another statement, Jesus spoke of the position of the man who divorced his wife: "Whosoever shall put away his wife, except it be for fornication, and shall marry another committeth adultery" (Matt. 19:9).

These two statements seem to allow divorce on the basis of unfaithfulness. However, in two other contexts, Jesus appears to give no sanction at all to divorce. In Mark 10:11-12 he said, "Whosoever shall put away his wife, and marry another, committeth adultery against her. And if a woman shall put away her husband, and be married to another, she committeth adultery." In Luke 16:18, Jesus makes a similar statement: "Whosoever putteth away his wife, and marrieth another, committeth adultery: and whosoever marrieth her that is put away from her husband committeth adultery."

How do Jesus' statements allowing divorce for infidelity harmonize with the statements that seem to forbid it entirely?

The first clue is found in Jesus' conversations with the Pharisees (Mark 10:5-9; Luke 16:18), in which He is making the point that divorce is contrary to God's plan for marriage. Even though the Law of Moses allowed divorce, it was only a provisional and reluctant allowance. Jesus put "teeth" into the Law by declaring that, even if the divorced couple had not been sexually unfaithful to each other, they would commit adultery in God's sight if they now married other partners.

Note that Jesus' statements belong in conversations with the Pharisees about the Mosaic Law, which they believed sanctioned divorce on grounds other than adultery (Deut. 24:1-4). Jesus' main point was that divorce should never be considered good, nor should it be taken lightly. So in His statement quoted in Luke 16:18, He did not even broach the subject of adultery. (Apparently, Mark 10:5-9 records only the words of Jesus that bore on the main point of the conversation.)

In the two passages from Matthew (one of them a fuller account of what is recorded in Mark 10), Jesus allows divorce for one reason only—"immorality," or illicit sexual intercourse. His thought is plainly that a person dissolves his marriage by creating a sexual union with someone other than the marriage partner. In that case, the decree of divorce simply reflects the fact that the marriage has already been broken. A man divorcing his wife for this cause does not "make her an adulteress," for she is one already. Divorce for unchastity usually frees the innocent partner to remarry without incurring the guilt of adultery (Matt. 19:9), but sometimes this is questioned.

Although Jesus allowed divorce for adultery, He did not require it. Just the reverse: Insisting that divorce disrupts God's plan for marriage, He opened the door to repentance, forgiveness, and healing in an unfaithful marriage, as He did in the case of other sin-racked relationships. Reconciliation was Jesus' way of solving marriage troubles.

God had demonstrated this way of reconciliation and forgiveness when He sent Hosea to marry a harlot, then told him to buy her back after she had sold herself to another man. God forgave Israel in just this manner When the people of Israel continued to worship idols, God sent them into captivity; but He redeemed them and brought them back again to Himself (Jer. 3:1-14; cf. Isa. 54).

C. Paul's Teachings. In 1 Corinthians 7:15, Paul says that a Christian whose mate has deserted the marriage should be free to formalize the divorce: " . . If the unbelieving depart, let him depart. A brother or a sister is not under bondage in such cases." [2] Yet Paul encourages the believer to keep the marriage together, in hopes that the unbelieving partner might be saved and the children will not suffer. Apparently, Paul is thinking of people who were married before they were converted, because he directs believers never to marry unbelievers (1 Cor. 7:39; 2 Cor. 6:14-18). Notice that this situation is quite different from the one Jesus addressed in the episode narrated in Matthew 19 and Mark 10. Jesus was speaking to the teachers of the Law—in fact, the misinterpreters of the Law—while Paul was speaking to Christians, many of them Gentiles who had never lived under the Law of

Moses. Paul's readers had changed their way of life since they had married, and were trying to influence their spouses to do the same. They were bound to think, not only of their own welfare, but of their spouses' and children's as well. For these reasons, and for the fact that monogamy is God's plan, marriages should be kept together.

Paul sought to discourage divorce; despite its undoubted commonness in the Graeco-Roman culture of pagan Corinth. In so doing, he showed himself to be a true and loyal spokesman of the Law.

4

BIRTH AND INFANCY

Today, as in biblical times, the birth of a child is a momentous occasion. But today's parents may well have debated questions that the people living in ancient Israel would have found strange and startling. For example, the following questions would not have entered the minds of the Israelites: "Should we have children?" "If so, should we limit the number to one or two?" Or, "If we do have children, when should we begin?"

The ancient Israelites' attitude could be summed up like this: "We want children. We want them now. We will have as many children as we can because children are very important to us. In fact, we would rather be 'wealthy' with children than with money."

THE DESIRE FOR CHILDREN

The very first command of God was, "Be fruitful and multiply, and replenish the earth and subdue it" (Gen. 1:28). The couples in biblical times took this command seriously. As one of the Jewish sages declared, "If anyone does not engage in increase, it is as though he were to shed blood or to diminish God's image."

God's command in Genesis 1:28 was viewed as a great privilege and blessing. The desire to fulfill this command is the subject of many stories in the Bible. Who can forget the son promised to Abraham in his old age (Gen. 15:4; 18:14), or the prophecy that Isaiah delivered to King Ahaz: "Behold, a virgin shall conceive, and bear a son, and shall call his name Immanuel" (Isa. 7:14). And then there was the most miraculous announcement of all, made to the Virgin Mary: "And, behold, thou shalt conceive in thy womb, and bring forth a son, and shall call His name Jesus" (Luke 1:31).

Every Jewish couple wanted children. In fact, that was the goal of marriage. The couple wanted to be remembered; only through offspring was this assured. To die without descendants might allow an entire family to be wiped out, forgotten forever. In 2 Samuel 14:4-7 we read about a widow with two sons. The sons got into a terrible argument and one killed the other. To make the guilty son pay for his crime, the rest of the relatives insisted that he should be executed. But the mother begged that his life be spared. She pleaded before the king: "And so they shall quench my coal which is left, and shall not leave to my husband neither name nor remainder upon the earth" (2 Sam 14:7).

Even today the Palestinian Arabs consider life to be unnatural without children. When a couple's first son is born, the father's name is enlarged so that the baby's name becomes a part of the father's name. For instance, a father whose son's name is "Daniel" becomes known as "Abu Daniel," meaning "Father of Daniel." And if a man has been married for a couple of years and his wife is not yet pregnant, he might very well be nicknamed "Father of Nothing."

Planning for children was a high priority in the Israelite couple's thinking. Even before the wedding, their relatives discussed the children that would be born to the marriage. The family of the bride met to pronounce a blessing on the bride, declaring their wish that she might have many children. We need only look at Genesis 24:60 to get a picture of this scene. Here we see Rebekah getting ready for the long journey back to Canaan to become Isaac's wife. Before she leaves, the family gathers around her to pronounce a blessing on her. The spokesman for the family says, "Thou art our sister, be thou the mother of thousands of ten thousands, and let thy seed possess the gate of those which hate them." A similar blessing was given to Ruth before her wedding to Boaz (Ruth 4:11-12, RSV).

A Jewish couple hoped that each new child would be a son,

but they gladly accepted either a boy or a girl. This was not the case in some of the surrounding cultures. Newborn girls were often left out in the open to die. Some gentile parents even sold their baby girls into slavery.

Jewish adults knew how a child was conceived, but they seldom discussed the sexual act itself. Instead, they emphasized that children were God's gift to the couple, "a heritage of the Lord" (Psa. 127:3). As the Psalmist declared, it is God the Lord "who dwelleth on high, who humbleth himself to behold the things that are in heaven, and in the earth: . . . He maketh the barren woman to keep house, and to be a joyful mother of children" (Psa. 113:5-6, 9).

The Bible uses many interesting figures of speech to describe a family. The mother is like a "fruitful vine" (Psa. 128:3). Children are like olive plants surrounding the parent tree (Psa. 128:3). Sons are like arrows in the hand of a warrior (Psa. 127:4).

THE CHILDLESS COUPLE

The story of Rachel and Leah (Jacob's wives) illustrates how important it was for a woman to give her husband sons (Gen. 30:1-24).

Many Israelite couples were unable to bear children. Today we know that couples may be childless because of the husband's or wife's sterility; but the world of the Bible blamed only the wife for the problem. (For an exception, see Deut. 7:14.)

Rachel's cry, "Give me children, or else I die!" (Gen. 30:1), expressed the feelings of every bride. And no doubt many a concerned husband agreed with Jacob's response: "Am I in God's stead, who hath withheld from thee the fruit of the womb?" (Gen. 30:2).

Townspeople ridiculed a barren woman by calling her a "reproach" (Luke 1:25). Even those who loved her treated her as an object of pity, and placed her in the same category as a widow.

But barrenness was more than a physical or social problem. Deep religious meanings were attached to the problem as well. Moses promised the people that if they obeyed the Lord, blessing would follow: "Thou shalt be blessed above all people: there shall not be male or female barren among you, or among your cattle" (Deut. 7:14). So barrenness was thought to be a result of disobeying God. This principle is seen throughout Israel's history. For example, Abraham openly declared to Abimelech, king of Gerar, that Sarah was his sister. But God revealed to Abimelech in a dream that Sarah was married. When the king returned Sarah to her husband, Abraham asked God to reward him with children. "For the Lord had fast closed up all the wombs of the house of Abimelech, because of Sarah Abraham's wife" (Gen. 20:18). This passage of Scripture describes a barrenness that lasted for only a short period of time. However, the condition could be permanent (cf. Lev. 20:20-21). But whether temporary or permanent, barrenness was thought to be the curse of God.

It is hard for us to imagine how devastating these events would have been for the childless wife. She was spiritually ruined, socially disgraced, and psychologically depressed. She was married to a husband who wanted a child to assure the continuation of his family line. That husband might continue to love her, but she felt that was small consolation (cf. 1 Sam. 1:6-8). It was in fact a great mercy, for a resentful husband could have made her life unbearable.

A barren couple spent a good deal of time examining their past failures to see if any sin had been unconfessed. Through tears the wife repented of all known sin. Then the husband offered a fitting sacrifice to cover any "unknown" sins (cf. Lev. 4:2). Childlessness became the main theme of the couple's prayers. Note how Isaac begged the Lord to let his wife bear a child (Gen. 25:21). Hannah sobbed before the Lord and promised that if God would give her a son, she would dedicate him to the Lord's service (1 Sam. 1:11).

When sin was ruled out as the cause of the problem, the wife was free to inquire about different kinds of remedies. Her relatives, friends, and neighbors might suggest that she

Mycenaean statuette. An old woman, a young woman, and a little boy are depicted in this ivory sculpture (thirteenth century B.C.). A close relationship between older and younger women was important in the ancient family structure, especially in the area of rearing children.

try various love foods or potions that had proved to be helpful to them. One such food is mentioned in Scripture: Rachel requested "mandrakes" from Leah, her sister (Gen. 30:14-16). Mandrakes were plants believed to produce fertility; they were often used as love charms. Rachel believed that if she ate this food she would conceive. In rabbinic times women sought to overcome their barrenness by changing their diets. Apples and fish were thought to cause a person to become sexually powerful for procreation.

Modern excavations in Israel have produced many clay fertility figures. They were supposed to help a woman get pregnant by "sympathetic magic." Each figurine was molded to look like a pregnant woman. As the barren woman handled it and kept it near her, she hoped to take on the likeness of the pregnant figure.

Women also wore amulets to insure fertility. Jeremiah the prophet noted another common heathen practice: The women of Judah kneaded cakes, gave drink offerings, and burned incense to the "queen of heaven" to assure fertility (Jer. 44:17-19; cf. Jer. 7:18). The "queen" mentioned in this passage was probably Astarte (Ashtoreth), the Canaanite goddess of sexual love, maternity, and fertility. Of course, all of these superstitious practices were evil in God's sight.

If all the remedies were unsuccessful, the woman was considered to be permanently barren. At this point, the husband might take drastic measures. He might marry another wife or (at least in patriarchal times) use a slave to bear children under his name. This is why Sarah gave her servant Hagar to Abraham (Gen. 16:2) and Rachel asked her husband Jacob to impregnate her handmaid, Bilhah (Gen. 30:3).

Adoption was also a method of overcoming the infertility of the wife. The childless couple could adopt an infant or even an adult as their own child. Eliezer of Damascus was a grown man, but Abraham told God that he was to be his heir (Gen. 15:2). The fifteenth-century B.C. tablets discovered at Nuzi show that Abraham was following a common practice for Semitic cultures, although we have few biblical references to it.

Mother and child. This crude clay figurine of a mother and her child, dating from about 3000 B.C., comes from Beth-Yerah in northern Israel. The family was a common subject of early Canaanite art.

Adoption solved many problems: The adopted son would care for the couple in their old age, provide them a proper burial, and inherit the family property. However, if the couple had a natural son after one had been adopted, he would become the rightful heir.

Note that after Bilhah's baby was born, it was placed in Rachel's lap. This act was the central part of the adoption ceremony. The baby was then adopted by Rachel as her own (cf. Gen. 30:3). The Bible's other references to adoption are in a foreign setting: Pharaoh's daughter adopted Moses (Exod. 2:10—Egypt) and Mordecai adopted Esther (Esther 2:7, 15—Persia).

Even with the emphasis on obtaining children, a few couples chose to die childless rather than resort to adoption or polygamy. This was the plan of Zechariah and Elisabeth (Luke 1:7).

If a woman became pregnant after long years of waiting, then she was likely to be the happiest woman in the village. There would be great rejoicing when her baby was born. We dramatically see this in the account of Elisabeth, the mother of John the Baptist. Luke writes, "And her neighbors and her cousins heard how the Lord had showed great mercy upon her; and they rejoiced with her" (Luke 1:58). When Rachel finally conceived and bore a son, she exclaimed, "God has taken away my reproach" (Gen. 30:23). In the hope that this would not be an only child, she called his name *Joseph* meaning "He adds," saying, "The Lord shall add to me another son" (Gen. 30:24).

MISCARRIAGE

Just as in our day, not all women in Bible times were able to carry the fetus long enough to give birth. Yet the Bible's references to miscarriage are of a general nature. Although the tragedy of miscarriage was probably whispered about in the women's circles, the people's sense of good taste probably kept them from discussing it openly.

Woman giving birth. The clay statuette from eighth-century Cyprus depicts a woman giving birth. The center figure, in labor, sits upright on the knees of her companion while a midwife attends to her. Some scholars think that Genesis 30:3 refers to this means of giving birth.

Sensing he was about to lose family, health and possessions, Job wished that he had been "as a hidden untimely birth . . . as infants which never saw light" (Job 3:16). The prophet Jeremiah bitterly professed that it would have been better if he had died in his mother's womb and had never been born (Jer. 20:17-18).

The women in Bible times would not have used modern medical terminology to describe miscarriage. They would have attempted to explain the miscarriage in other terms. They might trace the problem to a food that had been eaten or something that had been drunk. For example, during the days of the prophet Elisha, the women in Jericho were convinced that the water from the nearby spring was causing them to miscarry (2 Kings 2:19-20).

Sometimes miscarriage was caused by accident. A pregnant woman might be jostled or kicked by an animal. She might get caught between two men who were fighting. According to Mosaic Law, the person who inflicted the blow was fined if the mother miscarried. If the miscarriage caused complications and the woman died as a result, the Law exacted the death penalty (Exod. 21:22-23).

THE "BLESSED EVENT"

The Hebrews knew something about that growth process, even without current medical data at their fingertips. The Psalmist poetically described God's role in the process when he wrote: "For thou hast possessed my reins: thou hast covered me in my mother's womb. I will praise thee; for I am fearfully and wonderfully made: marvelous are thy works; and that my soul knoweth right well. My substance was not hid from thee when I was made in secret, and curiously wrought in the lowest parts of the earth. Thine eyes did see my substance, yet being unperfect; and in thy book all my members were written, which in continuance were fashioned, when as yet there was none of them" (Psa. 139:13-16).

A. Pain in Childbearing. The pharaoh of Egypt questioned two midwives because they disobeyed his order to kill the Hebrew male infants. They responded, ". . . The Hebrew women are not as the Egyptian women; for they are lively, and are delivered ere the midwives come in unto them" (Exod. 1:19).

How should we interpret what the midwives said? Were they just making up this story because they feared the Lord (Exod. 1:17)? And if they were telling the truth, what did they mean? We cannot assume that all Hebrew mothers had painless deliveries; other biblical passages do not back up this theory.

When Adam and Eve sinned against God in the Garden of Eden, part of God's curse on mankind was that women would experience pain in childbearing (Gen. 3:16). Birth pangs and the cries of a woman in labor were common in a Jewish village.

When the prophets sought to describe God's judgment, they often used the image of a woman in labor. For example, Isaiah said, "Like as a woman with child, that draweth near the time of her delivery, is in pain and crieth out in her pangs; so have we been in thy sight, O Lord. We have been with child, we have been in pain, we have as it were brought forth wind" (Isa. 26:17-18). Similarly, Jeremiah said, "For I have heard a voice as of a woman in travail, and the anguish as of her that bringeth forth her first child, the voice of the daughter of Zion, that bewaileth herself, that spreadeth her hands, saying, Woe is me now!" (Jer. 4:31).

Birth pains were sometimes accompanied by complications. The Old Testament records several occasions where the mother's life was endangered. For example, the child born to Tamar was named *Pharez,* meaning "breach." The midwife noticed that the child had made an unusually large breach or tear in the mother (Gen. 38:28). Jacob's beloved wife Rachel died while giving birth to Benjamin, her second son (Gen. 35:18-20). Also, Phinehas' wife lost her life in childbirth, though the child was saved (1 Sam. 4:20). The birth of a child was painful and often difficult. The mother suffered without benefit of modern painkillers or sophisticated medical assistance.

B. The Delivery. In some ancient cultures the mother would lie down to deliver a child; in others, the mother would squat in a crouching position. Although Scripture says little about this phase of birth, there is one reference to a birthstool (Exod. 1:16), which implies that the mother did not lie down. Unfortunately, the birthstool is not described. But such stools are well known from other cultures of the Middle East.

The mother was usually assisted by a midwife, a woman specially experienced in helping at the time of childbirth. Sometimes these women were mothers themselves; they had learned by experience what kind of assistance was needed. Some midwives were professional people who performed this service as a full-time occupation.

The midwife served several functions. In addition to delivering the baby, she advised and encouraged the woman in labor. On several occasions, Scripture records the words of midwives as they gave assurance and comfort (cf. Gen. 35:17; 1 Sam. 4:20). If twins were born, the midwife had the responsibility of making the distinction between the first- and second-born. As Tamar gave birth to her twins, the midwife took a scarlet thread and tied it on the hand of the firstborn, telling the mother, "This came out first" (Gen. 38:28).

The mother did not always have the benefit of a midwife. If she had a premature baby or was outside her normal surroundings, she might face this ordeal alone. Scripture suggests that Mary, the mother of Jesus, was alone with her husband when she gave birth to Jesus (Luke 2:7).

In biblical times the infant did not begin life in a sterile hospital setting. It was usually born at home, where the conditions were unsanitary. Probably it would be born on a dirt floor. Farm animals sometimes shared the same living quarters. The water used to cleanse the child was often polluted; the clothing used to wrap him had been washed in the same impure water. Disease-bearing flies and other insects quickly found the infant. The stable where Jesus was born may have been no worse than some of the homes in Bethlehem.

The newborn baby slept in the same bed as its mother, so that she could nurse it during its night feedings. However, this could result in tragedy. On one occasion, Solomon was asked to judge a case involving two harlots who lived in the same house. One of the women was a heavy sleeper, and during the night she accidentally rolled on her baby, which died. When she discovered the baby was dead, she secretly exchanged it with the other woman's. Solomon was able to determine which woman was the mother of the living boy (1 Kings 3:16-28).

Considering the poor living conditions, infant mortality must have been very high. Demographic studies in Egypt and other ancient cultures show that the infant mortality rate was as high as 90 percent. The many infant burial sites uncovered at various archaeological sites in Israel tend to support this assumption. Also, it is important to remember that the redemption ceremony of the firstborn male was not performed until the child was 30 days old. If he had survived the first month, his chances of growing to adulthood were good.

Immediately following the delivery, several tasks had to be performed. Until recently, a custom prevailed among the

Palestinian Arabs that may reflect the procedure in biblical times. First, the umbilical cord was cut and tied. Then the midwife picked up the baby and rubbed salt, water, and oil over its entire body. The infant was wrapped tightly in clothes or clean rags for 7 days, then the process was repeated. This continued until the child was 40 days old. The prophet Ezekiel mentioned salt, cleansing, and swathing bands in reference to the birth of a child (Ezek. 16:4). Luke noted that Mary "brought forth her first-born son, and wrapped him in swaddling clothes" (Luke 2:7).

The midwife's duties were finished when she handed the baby to the mother to be nursed. It was considered both a privilege and a duty for the Jewish mother to breast-feed her infant. Infants were actually breast-fed for their first year or more. But sometimes a mother was not physically able to nurse her child. When that happened, a wet nurse was secured. This wet nurse was another nursing mother (usually unrelated to the baby) who fed the baby her own breast milk.

Scripture relates something about three of these nurses. Pharaoh's daughter found the infant Moses among the reeds on the River Nile's bank. One of her first orders was to get a nurse from among the Hebrew women to nurse the child. Moses' wet nurse was his own physical mother (Exod. 2:7-8). The Bible describes a touching scene that shows the high esteem given these nurses: "But Deborah Rebekah's nurse died, and she was buried beneath Beth-el under an oak and the name of it was called Allonbachuth [or "Oak of Weeping"] (Gen. 35:8). Another wet nurse worked with the royal family in Jerusalem. She risked her life by hiding the young child, who was to inherit the throne when he was old enough to become king (2 Kings 11:1-3).

The midwife announced to the mother that the child had been born and was alive and well. If the father was at work in the field or market, she sent word to him. Jeremiah made reference to this practice when he said, "Cursed be the man who brought tidings to my father, saying, A man-child is born unto thee: making him very glad" (Jer. 20:15).

The family's neighbors would ask whether the newborn

child was a boy. The birth announcement was simple. It said, "There is a man child conceived" (Job 3:3), or "A man child is born unto thee" (Jer. 20:15). This reminds us of the announcement of the Messiah: "Unto us a child is born, unto us a son is given" (Isa. 9:6).

NAMING THE CHILD

Names were very important in the world of the Old Testament. Each Hebrew name had a meaning, and it became an important part of the infant's life. Jewish people believed that they must first know a person's name before they could know the person himself. We only have to look at the name *Jacob,* which means "heel grabber," to see the importance of a name. To know Jacob's name was to know his basic character! Therefore, the act of choosing a name for an infant was a serious responsibility.

After the Exile, the meaning of a name was of less importance. A child might be given the name *Daniel* not because of its meaning, but to honor the famous servant of God. But there were exceptions, even during this time. For example, the name *Jesus* is a Greek form of the Hebrew name *Joshua,* which means, "salvation of Yahweh."

The child's name was usually chosen by one or both parents. Scripture indicates that the mother usually named the infant. Just as today, other people took it upon themselves to assist in this important task. If Elisabeth's neighbors and kinsfolk had had their way, her son would have been named "Zechariah." But Elisabeth protested, insisting the boy would be called "John" (Luke 1:60-61).

Nowhere does Scripture specifically say when the child was to be named. In some instances, the mother named the child on the day of its birth (e.g., 1 Sam. 4:21). By New Testament times, the baby boy was usually named on the eighth day, at the time of his circumcision (cf. Luke 1:59; 2:21).

Most of the names in the Bible are *theophoric.* This means that a divine name was joined with a noun or verb, producing a sentence for a name. For example, *Jonathan* means "The Lord has given." The name *Elijah* refers to the prophet's loyalty: "My God [is] the Lord." This was true of many heathen names as well. Many names of the Old Testament contain the word *Baal.* King Saul's grandson was called Meribbaal (1 Chron. 8:34).

Circumstances surrounding the infant's birth sometimes influenced the choice of the child's name. For example, if a woman went to the well for water and had her baby there, she might call the child *Beera,* "[born at the] well." A baby born during a winter rainstorm might be called *Barak,* "lightning." When the Philistines captured the ark of the covenant from Israel, a mother was giving birth to a child. The baby was called *Ichabod;* in the words of the mother, "The glory [*chabod*] is departed from Israel" (1 Sam. 4:21).

Animal names were commonly used for children. *Rachel* means "sheep." *Deborah* is the Hebrew word for "bee." *Caleb* means "dog," and *Achbor* has reference to a "mouse." We can only guess why these animal names were used. Perhaps they expressed some type of parental wish. A mother might have called her newborn girl *Deborah,* desiring that she would mature into an industrious and busy "bee."

Akhnaton, Nefertiti, and children. This painted limestone plaque is a family portrait of Pharaoh Akhnaton (fourteenth century B.C.), his queen, and their three daughters. The queen sits holding two of the daughters, while the king hands an object to the eldest.

Often the name referred to a personality trait that the parents hoped would describe the child as he reached adulthood. Names like *Shobek* ("Preeminent") and *Azzan* ("Strong") can best be understood in this light. Yet in other cases, the name seemed to be the exact opposite of what the parents wanted the child to be. *Gareb* suggests a "scabby" condition and *Nabal* makes reference to a "fool." Some primitive cultures believed that demons want to possess attractive children, so they gave infants names that sounded distasteful. Perhaps names like "Scabby" and "Fool" were therefore given in biblical times to ward off evil spirits.

It is common today to name the firstborn son after the father, but that was not the case in biblical times. One has only to look through the various family trees described in the Scriptures to see this. For example, from Boaz to the last king of Judah, 24 names of kings are listed. And no two of them are alike!

Some names were more popular than others. For example, at least a dozen men mentioned in the Old Testament were called *Obadiah* ("servant of Yahweh"). In order to distinguish between many children having the same name, the name of the father might be attached to the son's name. The prophet Micaiah's expanded name was "Micaiah ben Imlah," or "Micaiah, the son of Imlah." The apostle Peter's name before Jesus changed it was "Simon Bar-Jona," or "Simon, the son of Jona." This custom also served to remind the son of his ancestors.

Another way to distinguish between people with the same name was to identify each person by the name of his hometown. David's father was called "Jesse the Bethlehemite" (1 Sam. 16:1). The giant that David killed was "Goliath of Gath" (1 Sam. 17:4). One of Jesus' loyal supporters was Mary Magdalene or "Mary of Magdala" (Matt. 28:1). Judas Iscariot, the disciple who betrayed Jesus, came from the town of Kerioth.

Sometimes the name of a person was changed after he reached adulthood. The individual himself might ask that his name be changed. Ruth's mother-in-law Naomi sought to have her name changed to *Mara* because, she said, "The Almighty has dealt very bitterly [*mara*] with me" (Ruth 1:20). Scripture does not say whether her neighbors took her seriously. The young Pharisee named Saul had been a Christian for years before he changed his name to Paul, after he converted an important official named Sergius Paulus on the island of Cyprus (Acts 13:1-13).

On other occasions, someone else gave a person a new name. An angel of the Lord gave Jacob his new name, *Israel* (Gen. 32:26). Jesus changed Simon's name to *Peter* (Matt. 16:17-18). It is uncertain how often people changed their name in biblical times.

RITUALS OF CHILDBIRTH

Ancient Jewish culture observed rituals in connection with childbirth. The Jewish child was born into a deeply religious community. The following rites had special religious meanings in the development of the child.

A. Circumcising the Males. Many cultures in the world today practice circumcision for hygienic reasons. Some primitive tribes perform the rite on infants and young boys, while others wait until the boys reach the age of puberty or are ready for marriage. These traditions have remained largely unchanged for centuries. Similar practices were common in the Near East in biblical times. Since the Philistines did not practice circumcision, the Jews ridiculed them (cf. 1 Sam. 17:26). In some cases, Israelites were circumcised as adults (Josh. 5:2-5).

Circumcision signified that the infant was being taken into the covenant community. The Lord said to Abraham, "He that is eight days old shall be circumcised among you . . . and my covenant shall be in your flesh for an everlasting covenant" (Gen. 17:12-13). Therefore, this practice was carefully observed. An uncircumcised person was considered to be heathen. When Greek culture came to Palestine two centuries before Christ, many Jews gave up their Jewish customs. Some

The Hebrew Midwife

A *midwife* is a woman who assists a mother in giving birth. In ancient times, a midwife's duties consisted of cutting the umbilical cord, washing the baby, rubbing it with salt, wrapping it in swaddling cloth, and then presenting it to the father. On one occasion a midwife suggested a name for the infant (Ruth 4:17). The skill and dedication of these women as they assisted at childbirth made theirs an honored profession. The midwife was often a friend and neighbor of the family, and sometimes one of the members of the household.

Midwifery is an ancient practice, first mentioned in the Bible during the time of Jacob (Gen. 35:17). The midwife was experienced in handling the difficulties associated with multiple births, as suggested when Talmar bore Pharez and Zarah (Gen. 38:27-30).

The Bible mentions two women who died during childbirth: Rachel as she bore Benjamin (Gen. 35:17), and Eli's daughter-in-law when Ichabod was born (1 Sam. 4:20-21). In each case the midwife's prompt announcement enabled the mother to name her son.

The two most famous midwives in the Bible are Shiphrah and Puah. They were believed to have been the chief midwives serving Hebrew women during the Egyptian bondage. Josephus and others believe these were Egyptian women whom Pharaoh trusted to carry out his orders to kill male babies of the Hebrews. But the midwives defied the Pharaoh with the excuse that Hebrews were more healthy and vigorous during childbirth than Egyptians. (This implied that it would be difficult for the midwives to claim that the babies died in childbirth.)

men submitted to an operation that made them appear "uncircumcised" again. This was tantamount to apostasy.

The Law of Moses did not stipulate who was to perform the operation on the infant. It is commonly assumed that an adult male cut off the infant's foreskin. On at least one occasion Scripture records that a woman did this; but the circumstances surrounding that particular event were unusual, for the husband seemed to be dying (cf. Exod. 4:25). The Hebrew word for "circumciser" and "father-in-law" is the same. This probably goes back to pre-covenant days when a young man was prepared for marriage by his future father-in-law.

Circumcision is an extremely delicate operation. In our society it is performed by a skilled physician. By New Testament times, the rite was probably performed by a specialist outside the family group (1 Macc. 1:61).

At first, crude instruments such as flint knives were used for this operation. Even after metal knives were developed, flint knives were used (Exod. 4:25 and Josh. 5:2). Slowly this tradition was given up, and by New Testament times flint knives had been replaced by metal ones.

The Jewish boy, as we saw, was to be circumcised on the eighth day. God first delivered this commandment to Abraham (Gen. 17:12) and repeated it to Moses in the wilderness (Lev. 12:3). In earlier periods, the Israelites did not always obey this command. But after the Exile, the law was carefully observed. This practice continued through New Testament times (cf. Luke 2:21) and remains a hallmark of Judaism today. When the eighth day fell on the Sabbath, the circumcision rite was still performed—in spite of many rules and regulations about suspending everyday activities that had been developed to keep the Sabbath holy.

Recent studies have confirmed that the safest time to perform a circumcision is on the eighth day of life. Vitamin K, which causes blood to coagulate, is not produced in sufficient amounts until the fifth to seventh day. On the eighth day the body contains 10 percent more prothrombin than normal; prothrombin is also important in the clotting of blood.

B. Purifying the Mother. Childbirth was thought to make a woman ceremonially unclean. That meant she was not allowed to participate in any religious observances or touch any sacred objects. Biblical scholars have long speculated about the reason for this. Did it emphasize that the child was born in sin? Did it demonstrate that sexual acts and the birth of a child were somehow sinful? Or was it designed simply as a protection for the mother, to keep her from feeling obligated to journey outside her home soon after the birth of a child? Scripture itself does not give us the reason. However, it is important to remember that anyone—man or woman—was considered ceremonially unclean if they had a discharge of blood, semen or pus (cf. Lev. 12; 15). Other cultures in biblical times had similar taboos.

According to Leviticus 12, the mother was unclean for 40 days after the birth of a son; she was unclean twice as long if a girl was born. Again, no reason is given.

At the end of this period, after the mother had presented a sin offering and a burnt offering at the central place of worship, she was pronounced ceremonially clean. This tradition is unusual, because sacrifices were normally presented by

Greek and Roman Schools

The ancient Romans and Greeks had a sophisticated system of schools. The schools were not compulsory, nor were they run by the government. Still, schooling was popular.

In the Greek system, boys were sent to school at age six. The school was owned and operated by the teacher. Apparently the Greeks did not have boarding schools.

The Greeks did not teach foreign languages. (They considered their language to be supreme!) Their education had three main divisions: music, gymnastics, writing. All Greek children were taught to play the lyre. Greek girls were taught to read and write by their mothers, who also taught them to weave, dance, and play a musical instrument. Oddly, the few well-educated Greek women were usually prostitutes for the wealthy.

Greek lecturers earned a living by teaching in school halls and even on the streets. Some of these wandering teachers—Socrates, for example—became famous. Greek boys could attend school until they were 16. After that, they were expected to train in sports.

Unlike the Greeks, the Romans used other nationalities to teach their children. Often a Greek nurse started a child's training. Boys and girls entered formal school at age seven. At 13, if they had done well, children went to high school; there were 20 such schools in Rome in A.D. 30. Even Roman secondary education was taught in Greek, and the teachers were generally Greek slaves or freedmen. Like the Greeks, the Romans had more advanced teachers who traveled from school to school.

the males. Also, the Law allowed the woman considerable freedom in choosing the type of animal she would sacrifice, depending upon her social status. A wealthy woman was expected to bring a lamb for a burnt offering; but if the family was extremely poor, even two turtledoves were allowed. It is interesting that Mary, the mother of Jesus, could afford only the pair of turtledoves at the time of her purification (Luke 2:22-24).

C. Redeeming the Firstborn. Since all firstborn were God's possession, it was necessary for the family to redeem, or buy back, that firstborn infant from God. The redemption price was 5 shekels of silver, given to the priests when the child was one month old (Num. 18:15-16).

Scripture doesn't tell us about the redemption ceremony itself, but by rabbinic times the following procedure had been established. The joyous occasion was celebrated on the thirty-first day of the child's life. (If the thirty-first day happened to fall on the Sabbath, the ceremony was delayed for one day.) The celebration took place in the infant's home, with a priest and other guests present. The rite began as the father presented the infant to the priest. The priest asked the father,

"Do you wish to redeem the child or do you want to leave him with me?" The father then answered that he would redeem the child, and he handed the 5 silver coins to the priest. As the infant was returned, the father gave thanks to God. The priest responded by declaring to the father, "Your son is redeemed! Your son is redeemed! Your son is redeemed!" After the priest pronounced a blessing on the child, he joined the invited guests at a banquet table.

If a child was an orphan at birth, the duty of redeeming him fell to one of the child's male relatives.

The child had survived those first critical weeks. His parents had named him and performed all the essential rites. The mother would continue to nurse the child until he was 2 or 3 years old. At that time, he would be weaned and would cross the line that separated infancy from childhood.

Statuette of pregnant woman. Women who could not conceive often kept fertility figures that looked like pregnant women. These figures were supposed to help produce pregnancy by "sympathetic magic." This ivory statuette depicts a pregnant woman with an exaggerated navel (*ca.* 3500 B.C.).

5

CHILDHOOD AND ADOLESCENCE

The people of Bible times respected their elders as a source of wisdom and guidance. They heeded God's command to "rise up before the hoary head, and honor the face of the old man . . ." (Lev. 19:32). Most of the community decisions were made by the village elders, and often these decisions affected the entire clan (cf. Exod. 3:16-18). The title of *elder* (actually meaning "bearded one") indicated a person's age. The Israelites believed that a person gained wisdom as he aged and was therefore a valuable asset to the family (Deut. 32:7; Ecclesiasticus 25:6).

We should remember this view of the elderly as we begin to study the children of biblical days. In our society, children are often the center of attention and activity. In ancient times, children were also important—but they could not challenge their parents or elders, nor could they freely express their opinions. Parents were determined to "train up a child in the way he should go" (Prov. 22:6). Part of the "way" was teaching

Childhood and schooling. A relief from a Roman sarcophagus shows the progress of a child from an infant nursing at his mother's breast (left) to a young boy ready for his first schooling (right).

children respect for their parents and elders. Even young adults did not challenge statements made by their elders. For example, Elihu began his speech to Job and his friends in an apologetic tone, saying, "I am young, and ye are very old; wherefore I was afraid and durst not show you my opinion" (Job 32:6). In this light, we can better understand why Jeremiah hesitated to become a prophet. He said, "Ah, Lord God! behold, I cannot speak: for I am a child" (Jer. 1:6). Jesus' disciples reflected this attitude when they attempted to shield Jesus from the children. But Jesus told them to "forbid them not, for of such is the kingdom of God" (Luke 18:16).

PHYSICAL APPEARANCE AND GROWTH

The Gospels give little information about the physical appearance of Jesus, either as an adult or as a child. But the Bible gives sketchy descriptions of some individuals. For example, David was described as being red-haired or ". . . ruddy, and withal of a beautiful countenance, and goodly to look to" (1 Sam. 16:12). However, we do not know what type of person the Israelites considered to be handsome.

Some murals and bas reliefs dating back to the time of the Old Testament show how the Israelites might have appeared. The problem here is that we cannot determine which features were real and which were imaginary. Still, they add one more piece to the puzzle.

Archaeological excavations give further evidence of the physical characteristics of the Israelites. We'll look at some of these clues below.

A. Growth Stages. The Hebrews used several words to describe stages of a child's growth. A very young child was called a "sucker," which meant that he was still nursing. Then he was referred to as a "weaned one"; this change was an important milestone in a child's life. When the child matured a bit more, the Hebrews said he was "one who takes quick little steps."

Another plateau was the reaching of puberty. A young

person at this stage was called an *elem* or *almah,* meaning "to be mature sexually."

Five stages of human life are outlined in Leviticus 27:1-8; three of these fit into the age of childhood or adolescence. The first stage was from birth until 30 days; the second stage was from one month to 5 years; and the third from 5 years until the age of 20. The last 2 stages were adulthood and old age.

B. Size. The Israelites considered themselves to be smaller than the Canaanites, who inhabited the Promised Land before them. When spies returned from scouting out the Promised Land, they reported that the land was filled with giants. They said, "The people is greater and taller than we; the cities are great and walled up to heaven; and moreover we have seen the sons of the Anakim there" (Deut. 1:28). The people referred to as "the Anakim" were legendary descendants of a tribe of giants. But archaeologists have found evidence that the Canaanites were of average size and build. It appears that the spies' report was based on fear rather than fact (Deut. 1:28; Num. 13:28).

By studying the skeletons of adult Israelites, scientists have found that their average size was from 160 to 170 cm. (63 to 67 in.). Their small size was due in part to the poor food source available to them. Drought and locust plagues reduced their crop production drastically. This caused widespread famine among their people (Amos 4:6-10).

In spite of all these hardships, there were a few overweight people. Eglon, King of Moab, is described as "a very fat man" (Judg. 3:17). But food was often scarce, so that while a rich man could buy more than he needed, a poor man would suffer near-starvation. Scripture condemns the callous selfishness of the rich (cf. Luke 12:13-21), as it does gluttony. For example, God judged Eli and his sons because they fattened themselves on the choicest parts of the offerings (1 Sam. 2:29).

Though the Israelites may have been smaller and thinner than their contemporaries, they were not weaker. Everyone worked hard, even the girls. Every day young women filled

Amenhotep III and family. This colossal family group 7 m. (23 ft.) in height depicts Pharaoh Amenhotep III (*ca.* 1450 B.C.) in ceremonial beard and headdress. Queen Tiy wears a heavy wig surmounted by a crown. Their three daughters are represented by the three small figures along the front of the throne seat. This indicates the insignificant role of children in Egyptian society.

their water jugs at the local well and carried them home on their heads. When filled with water, each jug weighed as much as 22 kg. (50 lb.). Preparing grain for food was another strenuous and backbreaking task. An ideal wife of that day was one with strong arms (Prov. 31:17).

Life demanded hard work on the part of the men; such work was part of a young boy's growing up too (1 Sam. 16:11). Both men and boys engaged in all sorts of physical labor. For example, they carried sick sheep or goats back to the village from faraway fields. When a house was to be built, they carried the stone with their hands. Most of their traveling was done on foot. All of this contributed to making the Israelites a strong and resilient people.

Sometimes a young man would demonstrate his strength and courage by attacking and killing a wild animal. David told

Saul, "Thy servant kept his father's sheep, and there came a lion, and a bear, and took a lamb out of the flock: and I went after him, and smote him, and delivered it out of his mouth; and when he arose against me, I caught him by his beard, and smote him, and slew him. Thy servant slew both the lion and the bear" (1 Sam. 17:34-36). Similar events are recorded throughout the Bible (e.g., 2 Sam. 23:20).

In every culture there are exceptions to the norm. The Bible says of Saul, "There was not among the children of Israel a goodlier person than he: from his shoulders and upward he was higher than any of the people" (1 Sam. 9:2). Goliath was also an exceptionally large man. In 1 Samuel 17:4, we read that his height was 6 cubits and a span. A *cubit* was the distance from the elbow to the tip of the middle finger, or roughly 45 cm. (18 in.). That would have made Goliath over 270 cm. (9 ft.) tall. At the other end of the scale was Zaccheus, who had to climb a sycamore tree to see over the heads of the crowd (Luke 19:3-4).

C. Color of Skin and Hair. The name *Esau* means "reddish-brown." The descendants of Esau were the reddish brown people called the Edomites. By contrast, the skin of the Israelites was lighter and more yellowish in color. In our day, Israelis seem to be dark-skinned people because of their constant exposure to the sun.

Young Israelite girls considered light skin to be beautiful, and they avoided the sun's rays as much as possible. We read in the Song of Solomon that the bride-to-be begged her handmaidens to "look not upon me, because I am black, because the sun has looked upon me" (Song of Sol. 1:6). She was embarrassed that her skin was not as light as the skin of the other girls.

The ancient Israelite youth had dark brown or black hair. Song of Solomon 5:11 describes it as "black as a raven." On several occasions in the Scripture, a youth's hair was likened to a flock of goats moving down a hillside (Song of Sol. 4:1; 6:5); the native goat was black.

Archaeologists have found headbands at various sites in Israel dating from Old Testament times. These relics indicate that men as well as women wore their hair long. Absalom (2 Sam. 14:26) and Samson (Judg. 16:16-19) both had long hair.

Canaanite parents often shaved the heads of their young sons, leaving a lock of hair on top (Lev. 19:27). This was an Egyptian custom but the Israelites were not allowed to do this. The apostle Paul urged women not to shave their heads and men not to wear long hair (1 Cor. 11:14-15); short hair implied that a woman was a prostitute. Hair styles were often a cultural matter; what one generation accepted, another did not.

D. Children with Physical Problems. Birth defects were prevalent in biblical times just as they are today. A list of some of the more common defects is found in the Pentateuch (Lev. 21:18-21). Apparently, a person with a birth defect was not allowed to perform any priestly duties. Such a person easily became the object of cruel jokes and teasing. This was strictly forbidden by God, who said, "Thou shalt not curse the deaf, nor put a stumbling block before the blind, but shalt fear thy God: I am the Lord" (Lev. 19:14; cf. Deut. 27:18).

EDUCATION

The Israelites provided a well-rounded education for their children. It included religious instruction as well as training in practical skills they would need for the workaday world. They were an agricultural people, so only the religious leaders were taught to read and write.

"Jesus increased in wisdom . . . and in favor with God and man" (Luke 2:52). This verse captures the goal of the Jewish educational system. It strove to impart not only knowledge but wisdom, centered around one's relationship with God.

In ancient Israel, education was an informal process. The parents did most or all of the training. There were no classrooms or structured curricula. By New Testament times, the Jews had adopted a more formal approach to education. They set aside classrooms and qualified teachers to instruct all the children in the village.

A. The Teaching Model. In order to understand the function of the Jewish teacher, we must first consider the divine Teacher after whom he modeled himself. Scripture refers to God as the Teacher who tells His students, "This is the way, walk ye in it" (Isa. 30:20-21). God knows and understands the needs of His students; He is fully versed in His subject; He is the perfect and infallible example for His students. The Jewish teacher had his pattern before him as he went to his work.

We know that God used men to teach the Law to the nation of Israel. These men were not only teachers but examples of godliness—men like Moses, the priests, and prophets such as Elijah. Their students were the adults of the nation of Israel, who were then responsible to pass the knowledge on to their children.

B. Parental Responsibility. The religious education of children was the parents' responsibility (Deut. 11:19; 32:46). No exceptions were made for parents who felt they were too busy to teach.

Even when children came of age and married, the parents' responsibility did not end; they also had an important part in educating the grandchildren (Deut. 4:9). In fact, they often lived in the same house.

Girls playing. Young girls dance and play games on this relief (*ca.* 2200 B.C.) from an Egyptian tomb at Sakkarah. Four of the girls hold mirrors.

Game from Tell Beit Mirsim.
Canaanite children played a game
on a board with ten playing
pieces—five in the form of a cone
and five tetrahedra, all of blue
earthenware. An ivory teetotum,
pierced on four sides with holes,
completes the set.

The Israelite father was ultimately responsible for the education of the children; but mothers also played a crucial role, especially until a child reached the age of five. During those formative years she was expected to shape the future of her sons and daughters.

When a boy became old enough to work with his father, the father became his principal teacher, even though the mother continued to share in the teaching responsibility (cf. Prov. 1:8-9; 6:20). The mother carried the main responsibility for her daughters, teaching them skills they would need to become in time good wives and mothers.

If someone other than the father had to assume the responsibility of teaching a boy, then that person was considered his "father." In later generations, a person who was specifically assigned to the task of teaching was called "father," and he addressed his pupils as "my sons."

The Jewish parents' major concern was that their children come to know the living God. In Hebrew, the verb "to know" means *to be intimately involved* with a person; Scripture stated that the reverence or "the fear of the Lord is the beginning of wisdom: and the knowledge of the Holy is understanding" (Prov. 9:10). Godly parents helped their children develop this kind of knowledge about God.

From earliest childhood, a youth learned the history of Israel. In early childhood, he probably memorized a creedal statement and recited it at least once a year, at the offering of the first fruits. The creed reduced the story of Israel's history to a simple form that was easy to memorize:

A wandering Aramean was my father; and he went down into Egypt and sojourned there, few in number; and there he became a nation, great, mighty, and populous. And the Egyptians treated us harshly, and afflicted us, and laid upon us hard bondage. Then we cried to the Lord the God of our fathers, and the Lord heard our voice, and saw our affliction, our toil, and our oppression; and the Lord brought us out of Egypt with a mighty hand and an outstretched arm, with great terror, with signs and wonders; and he brought us into this place and gave us this land, a land flowing with milk and honey. And behold, now I bring the first of the fruit of the ground, which thou, O Lord, hast given me (Deut. 26:5-10, RSV).

Thus the children learned that the nation of Israel had entered into a covenant with God. This covenant placed certain restrictions on them. They were not free to seek their own desires, but they had a responsibility to God because He had redeemed them. They were diligently taught the guidelines God gave them.

Jesus summarized the essence and intention of these laws when He declared, "Thou shalt love the Lord thy God with all thy heart, and with all thy soul, and with all thy mind. This is the first and great commandment. And the second is like unto it, Thou shalt love thy neighbor as thyself. On these two commandments hang all the law and the prophets" (Matt. 22:37-40).

There were probably no formal schools in Old Testament times. Most learning took place amid everyday life. As opportunities arose throughout the day, parents would instruct their children.

A child might ask, "Father, why are those stones piled there? What do they mean?" (cf. Josh. 4:21). A father would then take time to explain the religious background and significance of the monument.

The education of a child took a lifetime to complete. The Jewish family took seriously the Lord's instructions, ". . . These words, which I command you this day, shall be in thine heart: and thou shalt teach them diligently unto thy children" (Deut. 6:6-7). The phrase "to teach diligently" came from a Hebrew word that usually referred to sharpening a tool or whetting a knife. What the whetstone is to the knife blade, so training is to the child. Education prepared children to become useful and productive members of society.

C. Synagogue Schools. We are not sure when synagogue schools were first established. Some believe the practice dates back to the Exile in Babylon. Whenever it began, by New Testament times the synagogue school was a vital part of Jewish life.

Each Sabbath, Jews faithfully gathered at the synagogue to hear their rabbi read the Scriptures and explain the Law. This activity inspired the Muslims to nickname the Jews "the people of the Book." The synagogue sponsored special classes apart from the regular times of worship. During the week, boys came to these classes to study the Scriptures under qualified teachers. These classes supplemented the religious education the boys were receiving from their parents.

Jewish fathers were much more concerned with the character of a teacher than with his teaching ability. Naturally, they required him to be competent in his profession; but they were more concerned that he be a proper example to the children. Jewish writings from the New Testament era give us a partial list of the ideal characteristics of a teacher: He must not be lazy. He must have an even temper. He must never show partiality. He must never become impatient. He must never compromise his dignity by jesting. He must never discourage the child. He must show sin to be repulsive. He must punish all wrongdoing. He must fulfill all his promises.

Besides the reading of the Scriptures, Jewish boys were also taught etiquette, music, warfare, and other practical knowledge. We read how young David was said to be "cunning in playing [i.e., a musician], and a mighty valiant man, and a man of valor, a man of war, and prudent in matters, and a comely person, and the Lord is with him" (1 Sam. 16:18). We can tell from this account that David had a well-rounded education, as did most of the Jewish boys.

In New Testament times, the Jewish schools required each student to master several key passages of Scripture. Of primary importance was the *Shema,* another creedal statement of the Jews (Deut. 6:4-5). Next in importance were Deuteronomy 11:13-21 and Numbers 15:37-41. The student was also required to learn the *Hallel* ("praise") Psalms (Psa. 113–118), as well as the Creation story (Gen. 1–5) and the sacrificial laws (Lev. 1–8). If a child were unusually bright, he examined more of the Book of Leviticus.

Only the boys received formal training outside the home. They began by meeting in the teacher's house, where they read from scrolls containing small portions from the Scriptures, such as the *Shema.* This was the "elementary school" of the day.

When the boys were old enough to learn the sabbatical lessons, they met at the "house of the Book"—the synagogue. Here they entered the room where the Torah scrolls were kept and prepared their lessons under the supervision of the *Hazzan,* the keeper of the scrolls.

Later they were allowed to discuss questions of the Law with the Pharisaic teachers. These discussions constituted the "secondary" level of Jewish education.

In New Testament times, school was in session year-round. During the hot summer months the boys went to school no more than 4 hours a day. If it were an unusually hot day, school might be dismissed altogether. The class hours were before 10:00 A.M. and after 3:00 P.M. A 5-hour break occurred during the hottest part of the day.

The classroom contained a small raised platform where the teacher sat cross-legged. Before him on a low rack were scrolls containing selected Old Testament passages. There were no textbooks. The students sat on the ground at the teacher's feet (Acts 22:3).

Classes were not graded by age; all the students studied together in the same room. For this reason, their instruction had to be very individualized. The teacher copied down a verse for the younger students and they recited it aloud until they mastered it. Meanwhile the teacher helped the older boys read a passage from Leviticus. The noise probably would have been very distracting for us, but the Israelite boys soon became accustomed to it. The sages believed that if a verse were not repeated aloud, it would soon be forgotten.

D. Vocational Training. The boys must have been excited to follow their fathers into the fields to work or into the marketplace to buy and sell. They carefully observed their fathers planting, pruning, and harvesting. Sometimes they were allowed to attempt a difficult task, which added to the excitement. A new world had opened to a boy when he was old enough to go with his father.

But the work was monotonous and tiring. As the boy grew older, his responsibilities grew also. Before long, a son was expected to do a full day's work without stopping, other than to rest briefly.

Men encouraged their sons to work hard by admonishing them with Scripture. Proverbs 6:9-11 said, "How long wilt thou sleep, O sluggard? When wilt thou arise out of thy sleep? Yet a little sleep, a little slumber, a little folding of the hands to sleep: so shall thy poverty come as one that traveleth, and thy want as an armed man." To survive, a family had to work hard.

The Israelites believed that an undisciplined life would not prepare a youth to cope with what faced him. They taught their children the meaning of responsibility early in life, so when the youngsters reached adulthood they were able to meet its demands with confidence. If a son grew up irresponsibly, he not only embarrassed himself but brought shame to his family. One of the sages noted, "The rod and reproof give wisdom: but a child left to himself bringeth his mother to shame" (Prov. 29:15).

Since Israel had an agricultural society, much of the practical wisdom handed down from father to son revolved around farming. This included lessons on preparing the soil for planting and the cultivation of various crops, as well as harvesting and storing the bounty. Sons learned these skills by working alongside their fathers throughout their youth. Even when the Jewish people began to seek employment other than farming, they were still "people of the land."

It was also the father's responsibility to teach his sons a trade or craft. For example, if the father was a potter, he taught that skill to his sons. One of the Jewish sages affirmed that "he who does not teach his son a useful trade is bringing him up to be a thief."

While the boys were learning these skills, the girls learned baking, spinning, and weaving under the watchful eyes of their mothers (Exod. 35:25-26; 2 Sam. 13:18). If there were no sons in the family, daughters might be required to learn the father's work (Gen. 29:6; Exod. 2:16).

Circumcision. This relief at Sakkarah depicts the Egyptian rite of circumcision. To the left, an assistant holds the boy's hands while the circumcisor performs the operation with a rounded object, perhaps a flint knife (cf. Exod. 4:25). To the right, the patient braces himself by placing his hand on the head of the circumcisor. Unlike Egyptians, the Hebrews circumcised male infants at the age of eight days, to signify the child's acceptance into the covenant community.

LEISURE ACTIVITIES

Young people in biblical times did not have the "time on their hands" that youths have today. But they still had plenty of time for recreation and leisure.

A. Toys. Young people had few toys. They generally amused themselves by playing with a stick, a bone, or a piece of broken pottery. Terra cotta toys have been found in many excavations.

In Egypt, archaeologists have found simple mechanical toys such as carts and wagons in the royal tombs. Israelite girls played with simple clay dolls clothed with rags.

On one occasion, the prophet Isaiah likened God to a person hurling a ball (Isa. 22:18). This is the only biblical reference to such a toy. Unfortunately, the prophet described neither the ball nor the game that was played with it.

B. Games. The prophet Zechariah foretold times of peace for Israel by saying, ". . . The streets of the city shall be full of boys and girls playing . . ." (Zech. 8:5). Scripture does not describe the games children might have played, but it does mention their dancing and singing (cf. Job 21:11-12). Jesus said the people of His generation were "like unto children sitting in the market, and calling unto their fellows, And saying, We have piped unto you, and ye have not danced; we have mourned unto you, and ye have not lamented" (Matt. 11:16-17).

Drawings on the walls of ancient Egyptian tombs show children wrestling and playing games such as tug of war. Although there is little evidence that Hebrew boys played these sports, it is highly probable. Footraces and hopscotch were also games children enjoyed.

Boys of biblical times loved to explore the caves and crevices that surrounded their world. Shepherd boys often sneaked off to explore or trap wild animals. The boys also practiced using a sling or throwing a spear. Even in play, boys were preparing themselves for manhood.

GOING UP TO JERUSALEM

The Lord commanded all of the adult Hebrew males to congregate regularly at a central place of worship (Exod. 23:14-17; Deut. 16:16-17). The purpose was primarily religious, but the children considered the trip to be a kind of vacation, full of adventure and excitement. They counted it a privilege to go. Jerusalem was full of new sights and sounds that they were eager to experience. Often the children became so anxious to reach Jerusalem that they ran ahead of the slower adults.

THE EVENING CIRCLE

The evening meal in a Jewish village was eaten about two hours before sundown. Afterward, all of the men gathered in an open-air meeting place, where they sat or lay in a large circle with the older or more respected men in the center. On

Game board. Discovered in a grave at Ur, this game board (*ca.* twenty-fifth century B.C.) was hollowed out to contain the fourteen round playing pieces. The board is inlaid with shell, bone, red limestone, and strips of lapis lazuli set in bitumen.

the outer edges the older boys could stand and listen as the men related the events of that day or long ago.

The circle served as the evening "newspaper." We know what sort of things took place. The men discussed such things as the birth of a child, the illness of a villager, the appearance of a lion or bear in the vicinity, or national events. Then their thoughts probably turned to plans for the future. They might discuss the prospect of a bountiful harvest, the first signs of a plague of locusts, or the amount of rain that had fallen.

Silence then would reign for a few moments, after which an old man might begin to recite a poem of heroic deeds long ago, like the story of David. This might lead to a song, with many of the men joining in. Then a voice might declare in proverbial style, "Under three things the earth trembles." Another man across the circle might respond with, "Under four it cannot bear up." Then different men would list four things that the earth could not bear, like "a slave when he becomes a king." After a period of laughter and reflection, one and then another would offer vivid comments on life, such as, "Like a potsherd covered with silver dross . . .," followed by, "[are] burning lips and a wicked heart" (Prov. 26:33). It was a strange and wondrous type of conversation—shrewd, witty, weighty, and most instructive. This type of dialogue might have continued for several rounds before the topic changed and the meeting closed.

We can imagine that as the young men walked home, each reflected on what he had heard. Some stored important information they wanted to remember. Others found their hearts strangely stirred by the tales of daring men of old. Others had simply been entertained by the gossip and proverbs they had heard. But collectively their stock of wisdom and insight had increased, and so their lives had been enriched.

6

DISEASES AND HEALING

Disease and sickness have plagued man since God cast Adam and Eve out of the Garden of Eden (cf. Gen. 2:19). The Hebrews believed that illness was caused by sin in the individual, which God had to punish (Gen. 12:17; Prov. 23:29-32), the sin of a person's parents (2 Sam. 12:15), or seduction by Satan (Matt. 9:34; Luke 13:16). However, some scriptures show that there is not always such a simple explanation for disease (cf. Job 34:19-20).

Even in Old Testament times, the Hebrews associated healing with God. For example, Malachi spoke of the Sun of Righteousness rising with healing in his wings (Malachi 4:2), and David praised God as the One "that healeth all thy diseases" (Psa. 103:3).

RITUAL CURES AND MIRACULOUS HEALINGS

Here we will review some of the diseases and related problems of Bible times. An understanding of these problems is important for every Bible student, because they often affected the course of Israel's history, and Jesus' ministry emphasized the healing of the sick.

A. Aphasia. This is the temporary loss of speech, usually caused by a brain lesion but sometimes attributed to an emotional upset. This happened to the prophet Ezekiel (Ezek. 33:22). When an angel told Zechariah that he was going to be the father of John the Baptist, the old man came out of the temple and could not speak (Luke 1:22).

B. Apoplexy. This term refers to a rupture or obstruction of a brain artery, causing a stroke. When Abigail told Nabal of his insult to David and its dire consequences, Nabal's "heart died within him, and he became like a stone"; 10 days later he died (1 Sam. 25:37-38). These symptoms suggest that he suffered an attack of apoplexy. The same fate may have befallen Uzzah, who touched the ark of the covenant (2 Sam. 6:7), as well as Ananias and Sapphira (Acts 5:5, 9-10).

C. Blains. This term from the KJV probably refers to anthrax, a disease that can be transmitted to humans by cattle, sheep, goats and horses. The disease is caused by a rod-shaped bacterium that forms spores. These spores, in turn, can infect humans, who develop a boil-like lesion with a *pistule* (blain). In the infective stage, the blain is called a *malignant pistule*. Blains are mentioned only once in the Bible (Exod. 9:9-10). God inflicted them on the Egyptians when the pharaoh refused to let the Hebrews go to the Promised Land.

D. Blemishes. This general term refers to any bodily defect such as blindness, lameness, a broken bone, extra fingers or toes *(polydactylism)*, a humped back and so on. A person with blemishes could not offer sacrifices to God (Lev. 21:16-24), nor was he permitted to go beyond the veil of the temple or come near the altar, for this would defile the sanctuary. Imperfect animals could not be used for sacrifices (Exod. 12:5).

E. Blindness and Hearing Loss. Three types of blindness are mentioned in Scripture: sudden blindness caused by flies and aggravated by dirt, dust, and glare; the gradual blindness caused by old age; and chronic blindness. Paul suffered temporary blindness on the road to Damascus (Acts 9:8). Scripture often refers to old persons whose eyes "grew dim" (cf. Gen. 27:1; 48:10; 1 Sam. 4:15). But the Bible more often refers to chronic blindness.

The Israelites had compassion for the blind. In fact, God placed a curse upon those who made the blind wander out of their way (Deut. 27:18). Jesus ministered to many people who were blind. He said, "[God] has anointed me to preach the gospel to the poor. He has sent me to heal the broken-hearted, to preach deliverance to the captives, and recovering of sight to the blind" (Luke 4:18). Jesus healed a man born blind (John 9:1-41); a blind man whose healing was gradual

Christ healing a blind man. In this detail from the front of a Roman sarcophagus (*ca.* A.D. 330), Christ touches the eyes of a blind man with a paste of spittle before sending him to the Pool of Siloam (John 9). The Hebrews believed that God would curse those who made the blind to wander out of their way (Deut. 27:18).

(Mark 8:24); two blind men sitting by the wayside (Matt. 20:30-34); and a great number of others (Mark 10:46-52; Luke 7:21).

Blindness was often understood to be a punishment for evil-doing. We find examples of this at Sodom (Gen. 19:11); in the Syrian army (2 Kings 6:18); and in the case of Elymas at Paphos (Acts 13:6-11).

The New Testament occasionally refers to persons who had lost the ability to speak (cf. Matt. 9:32; 15:30; Luke 11:14). This often was the result of hearing loss.

F. Boils. This term refers to any inflamed ulcers on the skin, such as those caused by a staph infection. They may have been confused with "blains" or anthrax. Boils ("shechin" in Hebrew) are first mentioned in Exodus 9:9, when the pharaoh refused to let the Israelites leave Egypt, and boils broke out upon the people. Satan was permitted to afflict Job with boils from the top of his head to the tip of his toes (Job 2:7). King Hezekiah also was afflicted with boils (2 Kings 20:7), which Isaiah cured by applying a poultice of figs. A fresh fig poultice has a drawing effect. Before the advent of antibiotics, this type of treatment for boils was common.

G. Cancer. Hezekiah was very sick and the Lord told him to prepare to die (2 Kings 20:1). The Lord inflicted an incurable disease upon Jehoram, and after two years his bowels fell out (2 Chron. 21:18-19). Bible scholars believe these men may have suffered some type of cancer, though chronic dysentery would also have produced Jehoram's symptoms. However, the Bible does not refer to the cancer by name because the disease had not been identified in biblical times.

H. Consumption or Tuberculosis. Moses warned the rebellious Israelites. "The Lord shall smite thee with a consumption, and with a fever, and with an inflammation and with an extreme burning . . ." (Deut. 28:22). The KJV uses the word *consumption* to refer to tuberculosis, a consumptive infection of the lungs.

I. Dysentery. This is a disease that in its advanced stage, rots the bowels (2 Chron. 21:15-19). The fibrine separates from the inner coating of the intestines and is expelled.

The New Testament refers to a severe form of dysentery as the "bloody flux." The father of a Christian named Publius lay sick with the bloody flux (Acts 28:8). Paul came in and prayed for him and the man was healed.

J. Edema ("Dropsy"). This describes an abnormal accumulation of serous fluid in the body's connective tissue or in a serous cavity and is a symptom. The accumulation causes swelling. Jesus met at least one victim of edema in a certain Pharisee's house. Asked by Jesus if he thought it lawful to heal on the Sabbath, the Pharisee declined to answer. Jesus thereupon healed the sufferer (Luke 14:1-4).

K. Endocrine Disturbances. The Law of Moses did not permit a dwarfed person to enter the congregation of God's people (Lev. 21:20). Modern science has shown that dwarfism is caused by disturbances in the endocrine glands.

The Bible also mentions a number of giants, such as Goliath (1 Sam. 17:4). True giantism is caused by excessive secretions of the pituitary gland. However, many tall persons inherit their tallness from their forebears.

L. Epilepsy. This is a disorder marked by erratic electrical discharges of the central nervous system and manifested by convulsive attacks. A certain man brought his epileptic son to Jesus for help (Mark 9:17-29). The KJV says that the boy had a "dumb spirit." Jesus healed him.

An ancient theory held that epilepsy was caused by the moon; people referred to epileptics as being "moonstruck." Psalm 121:6 may reflect this idea when it says, "The sun shall not smite thee by day, nor the moon by night."

M. Female Disorders. According to the Mosaic Law, a woman suffering from menstrual disorders was to be considered unclean (Lev. 15:25). One such woman who had suffered for 12 years (Luke 8:43-48) touched the hem of Jesus' garment and, because of her great faith, was healed immediately.

N. Fevers. The KJV uses the word *ague* to describe a burning fever. Moses warned the rebellious Israelites that "I will ever appoint over you terror, panic, consumption and the burning ague that shall consume the eyes" (Lev. 26:16). Deuteronomy 28:32 also refers to ague.

When Jesus found Simon Peter's mother-in-law ill with this symptom, He rebuked the fever and she was able to rise from her bed and wait on the disciples (Luke 4:38). On another occasion, Jesus healed the feverish son of a government official (John 4:46-54).

Many diseases in ancient Palestine would have been characterized by high fevers, the most common of which were malaria and typhoid. A plague broke out when the Philistines placed the ark of God in an idol's temple (1 Sam. 5:2, 9, 12). The outbreak was associated with mice.

O. Gangrene. This disease is mentioned only once in the Bible: "And their word will eat as doth a canker" (2 Tim. 2:17). Here the KJV translates the Greek *gaggarina* as *canker.* It refers to the circulatory deterioration that we commonly call *gangrene,* which spreads rapidly and eats up tissue.

P. Gout. Excessive uric acid in the blood causes this kidney ailment that manifests itself through painful inflammation of joints. Second Chronicles 16:12-13 says that King Asa had a foot disease, which apparently was gout.

Q. Lameness. Scripture describes many persons who were lame, the most memorable case being recorded in Acts 3:2-11, where we read about a man (born lame) who was carried daily to Jerusalem's Beautiful Gate to beg. One day the beggar saw Peter and John entering the temple and beseeched them for money. Instead, the apostles invoked the name of Jesus to heal the man. Peter lifted up the beggar, who began to walk. Jesus healed many persons who were lame (cf. Matt. 15:30-31).

R. Leprosy. One of the most dreaded diseases of the

The Leper

Throughout history, leprosy has been one of mankind's most feared diseases. Until this century, men have relied upon various forms of social ostracism in an effort to control the disease. The Hawaiians banished lepers to the island of Molokai. Medieval nobles constructed vast leprosariums. And the ancient Jews cast the leper "without the camp" (Lev. 13:46).

We have little evidence of the actual lives of lepers in biblical times after they had been segregated from the community. Leviticus 13–15 contains the most relevant data on the treatment—or lack thereof—of leprosy in the Old Testament. These chapters mainly detail the symptoms of the disease, the procedures by which a priest determined a case that was cured, and the offerings to be made before the leper could reenter the community.

The leper's condition of life was very simply described in Leviticus: "And the leper in whom the plague is, his clothes shall be rent, and his head bare, and he shall put a covering upon his upper lip, and shall cry, Unclean, unclean. All the days wherein the plague shall be in him he shall be defiled; he is unclean: he shall dwell alone; without the camp shall his habitation be" (Lev. 13:45-46).

It was a fearsome fate to be condemned to the life of the leper. In medieval times, a priest would often read the burial service over a leper before he was cast out of the city. The miracles of Christ in curing lepers are testimony to His compassion as well as His power (cf. Matt. 8:1-4; Mark 1:40-45; Luke 5:12-14).

Luke is the only Gospel writer to tell of Jesus' cure of ten lepers during His last journey to Jerusalem. Ten found themselves cured on the way to see the priest, but only one returned to thank Christ. This story is the sole New Testament evidence that lepers congregated together, suggesting that the law of Leviticus had been relaxed. Second Kings 7:3-10 mentions four lepers huddling together outside the gates of a city. But apparently lepers were segregated from the healthy population of towns. In Old Testament times, leprosy was considered a source of physical contamination rather than of moral corruption (which was a popular myth in Jesus' time).

Leprosy was always a disaster, but it took centuries for society to learn how to cope with the disease.

world, leprosy is caused by a bacillus and is characterized by formation of nodules that spread, causing loss of sensation and deformity. Now treated with sulfone drugs, leprosy is perhaps the least infectious of all known contagious diseases. Hansen's Disease, as it is more properly known, was often misdiagnosed in biblical times. People believed then that it was highly contagious and hereditary. Leviticus 13:1-17 condemned leprosy as a "plague."

On the basis of a hair in a scab, a pimple, or a spot on the skin that had turned white, the priest would declare a person to be a leper and would quarantine him for 7 days. If no change in the spot occurred by then, the quarantine would be extended another week. At that time, if the spot had started to fade, the "leper" would be pronounced cured and returned to his normal life. However, if the spot remained or had spread, he was declared unclean and banished.

Leprosy was very common in the Near East. If a Hebrew was healed of leprosy, he was expected to offer certain sacrifices and engage in rites of purification (Lev. 14:1-32). Jesus healed lepers on numerous occasions (cf. Luke 5:12-13; 17:12-17).

S. Malaria. This infectious disease was caused by protozoa of the genus *plasmodium*. These one-celled animals can live in the blood of human beings and animals or in the female *Anopheles* mosquito. Once malaria is in the system, it recurs. Paul may have been referring to malaria when he spoke of his "thorn in the flesh" (2 Cor. 12:7).

T. Mental and Nervous Disorders. King Saul seems to have had symptoms of manic depression (cf. 1 Sam. 16:14-23), and the Bible mentions others who may have suffered from mental or nervous disorders. King Nebuchadnezzar is an example (Dan. 4:33).

U. Palsy. The KJV uses this term to refer to total paralysis. The Gospels record a well-known incident in which Jesus healed a paralyzed man at Capernaum (Mark 2:1-12). The Book of Acts describes how the apostles healed people with "the palsy" (Acts 8:7; 9:33-34).

V. Plague. Our English versions may use this word to

denote any epidemic disease. It is also used in a general sense in Exodus 7–10, where it refers to the hardships that God inflicted upon the Egyptians.

Epidemics hit the Israelites three times during their wandering in the wilderness. The first time was when they were eating the quail that God sent to satisfy their longing for meat (Num. 11:33). The second time, a "plague" claimed the lives of spies who discouraged the Israelites from entering the Promised Land (Num. 14:37). The third epidemic came as God's punishment upon the Israelites. Aaron stopped this "plague" by offering incense to God (Num. 16:46-47). On one other occasion, Phinehas saved the Israelites from an epidemic by killing a man who brought a Midianite woman into their midst. Nevertheless, 24,000 people died (Num. 25:8-9).

The Old Testament describes many cases in which God sent "plagues" to chastise His people. One example is found in 2 Samuel, where David says, "Build an altar unto the Lord that the plague may be stayed from the people" (2 Sam. 24:21).

The KJV also uses *plague* to refer to any painful affliction. When the woman with a chronic hemorrhage was healed, she felt that she had been healed of a "plague" (Mark 5:29). We have no evidence that the Bible ever refers to bubonic plague, which would claim millions of lives in medieval Europe.

W. Polio. This is the common name for infantile paralysis, which usually affected children. First Kings 17:17 tells of a woman who brought her son to the prophet Elijah. The boy was so sick that there was no breath in him; this symptom suggests that he may have had polio, although it also may have been a form of meningitis. Elijah revived the boy through the Lord's intervention in answer to his prayer. However, Scripture does not tell us if the boy was completely cured. The men described in Matthew 12:9-13 and John 5:2 may have had polio.

X. Skin Disorders. The Bible refers to many kinds of skin disorders such as the "itch" (KJV) or ringworm (Lev. 13:30; 21:20). Leviticus 13:39 probably refers to vitiligo, which was confused often with leprosy.

When the KJV uses the word *scurvy,* it is not referring to the vitamin deficiency that causes the problem known by that

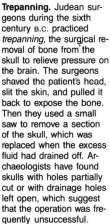

Trepanning. Judean surgeons during the sixth century B.C. practiced *trepanning,* the surgical removal of bone from the skull to relieve pressure on the brain. The surgeons shaved the patient's head, slit the skin, and pulled it back to expose the bone. Then they used a small saw to remove a section of the skull, which was replaced when the excess fluid had drained off. Archaeologists have found skulls with holes partially cut or with drainage holes left open, which suggest that the operation was frequently unsuccessful.

name today. Instead, the reference is to an itching or scaling condition caused by a fungus (Lev. 21:20, 22).

Y. Smallpox. Some Bible scholars believe that the Hebrew word *maqaq* (literally "waste away") refers to smallpox. The KJV usually translates this word as "pine away," which suggests emotional despair: "And they that were left of you, shall pine away" (Lev. 26:39). "Ye shall not mourn nor weep, but ye shall pine away for your iniquities" (Ezek. 24:23). In one instance, the KJV understands *maqaq* to denote a "corruption" of the skin: "My wounds stink and are corrupt because of my foolishness" (Psa. 38:5).

Z. Sunstroke. Isaiah may have referred to sunstroke or heat prostration when he said, "Neither shall heat nor sun smite thee" (Isa. 49:10). Second Kings describes a young man who was working among the reapers when he said to his father, "My head, my head." He was carried into the house, where he died (2 Kings 4:18-20). We would assume that sunstroke was a common malady in the hot summers of the Near East.

AA. Syncope. Arrested heart action or the sudden lowering of blood pressure is normally called *syncope*. When Jacob learned that his son Joseph was still alive, his heart "fainted" (Gen. 45:26)—probably a reference to syncope. When Eli heard that the ark of the covenant had been captured, he fell backwards off his seat, broke his neck, and died (1 Sam. 4:18). This may have been another instance of heart failure or syncope.

BB. Veneral Disease. There is some evidence that veneral diseases were common in Bible times. For example, Zechariah 11:17 warns the shepherd who leaves his flock, saying that his arm will be dried up and his right eye will go blind. These symptoms indicate a disease of the spinal cord, probably a venereal disease. Leah had an eye condition that could have been the result of hereditary syphilis (Gen. 29:17).

CC. Worms. Isaiah warned that the rebellious people of Israel would be afflicted with worms (Isa. 51:8). He also predicted this fate for Babylon (Isa. 14:11). This parasitic disease could be fatal because no medical remedies were available.

Scripture says that "an angel of the Lord" smote Herod the Great. Worms ate him up and he died (Acts 12:23).

THE USE OF MEDICINE

When a person's body began to deteriorate and suffer pain, the victim would naturally look for a remedy. Thus the people of ancient times developed an extensive knowledge of natural medicines.

Probably the first medicines were introduced to the Israelites through the Egyptian people, especially the priests. Egyptians also embalmed their dead with spices and perfume—a custom that the Israelites soon came to accept.

In Bible times, medicines were made from minerals, animal substances, herbs, wines, fruits, and other parts of plants. Scripture often refers to the medicinal use of these substances.

For example, the "balm of Gilead" is mentioned as a healing substance (Jer. 8:22). The "balm" is thought to have been an aromatic excretion from an evergreen tree or a form of frankincense. Wine mixed with myrrh was known to relieve pain by dulling the senses. This remedy was offered to Jesus as He hung on the cross, but He refused to drink it (Mark 15:23). The Israelites anointed their sick with soothing lotions of olive oil and herbs. In the story of the Good Samaritan, oil and wine were poured into the wounds of the beaten man (Luke 10:34). The early Christians continued this practice, anointing the sick as they prayed for them (James 5:14).

Matthew 23:23 mentions certain spices as antacids. Mandrakes were used to arouse sexual desires (Gen. 30:14). Other plants were used as remedies or stimulants.

PHYSICIANS AND THEIR WORK

Professional physicians practiced their skills in Bible times, but their work was largely considered to be magical. The Old Testament does not mention the names of any physicians, though it often refers to their work (cf. Gen. 50:2; 2 Chron. 16:12; Jer. 8:22). The deuterocanonical book of Ecclesiasticus (second century B.C.) celebrates the wisdom and skill of physicians (38:1-15). In the New Testament, Luke is mentioned by name as the "beloved physician" (Col. 4:14).

Circumcision is the only type of surgery mentioned in the Bible. This was the ceremonial removal of the foreskin of the male Hebrew child 8 days after birth. The practice was begun at God's command by Abraham (Gen. 17:10-14), and God showed anger with Moses for his failure to observe it (Exod. 4:24-26). Even Jesus was circumcised when He was 8 days old (Luke 2:21).

RITUAL CURES AND MIRACULOUS HEALINGS

The Bible refers to some cases in which an ailing person performed a ritual washing in order to receive a cure. When Naaman contracted leprosy, for example, the prophet Elisha instructed him to submerge himself seven times in the Jordan

River. Naaman did so and was healed (2 Kings 5:10). Jesus applied mud to the eyes of a blind man and told him to wash it off in the pool of Siloam. The blind man obeyed and received his sight (John 9:7).

On many more occasions, God performed miracles through the ministry of His servants. Elijah and Elisha saw numerous cures of this kind (cf. 1 Kings 17:17-22; 2 Kings 4:32-37). When Jesus cured people of all manner of diseases, it confirmed that He was the Messiah (Luke 7:20-22).

The temple priests had several medical functions. Leviticus describes seven forms of ritual purification that had medical significance. They deal with: post-childbirth (Lev. 12), leprosy (Lev. 13), venereal disease (Lev. 15:12-15), the male sexual function (Lev. 15:16-18), sexual intercourse (Lev. 15:18), menstruation (Lev. 15:19-30), and dead bodies (Lev. 21:1-3).

Surgeon's tools. Knives, scalpels, tweezers, and clamps are among these surgeon's tools found at Pompeii. They indicate that surgical arts were quite sophisticated by the first century A.D.

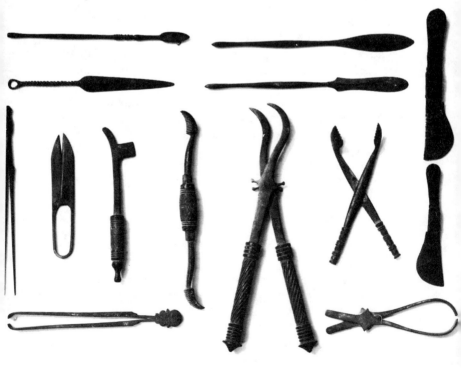

7

FOOD AND EATING HABITS

From Genesis 1:29 (when God said, "I have given you every herb bearing seed, which is upon the face of the earth . . . ; to you it shall be for meat") to Revelation 22:2 (when John tells about the "tree of life which bare twelve manner of fruits") the Bible is packed with references to food.

Vegetable products formed a major portion of the diet in the warm climate of Palestine. When meat was used, it was often for the purpose of serving strangers or honored guests.

Grains were an important part of the diet. Bread was eaten by itself or with something to increase its flavor, such as salt, vinegar, broth, or honey. Fruits and fish were a favorite part of the diet. Recall the disciples who were called from their fishing nets by Jesus.

The serpent tempted Eve to eat a piece of fruit, and sin entered the world. Esau sold his birthright for a mess of pottage. Jesus was tempted to turn stones into bread, and He used food—bread and wine—as a symbol of our participation in His suffering. Food—an earthy, human necessity—is a fascinating thread woven through the story of God's revelation to humankind.

EATING CUSTOMS

Scripture is filled with references to banquets and feasts; very little is said about day-to-day family meals. All evidence, however, points to the custom of two regular meals a day—breakfast, a light meal in the morning, and supper, a heavier meal in the evening when the air was cooler.

Earlier Jews sat on mats on the floor to eat. However, they

later adopted the custom of using a table with couches on which they reclined (John 21:20). A short prayer or blessing was offered before eating, as when Jesus blessed the bread when he fed the multitude (Matt. 14:19). Washing one's hands was considered essential and was observed as a religious duty, especially by the Pharisees (Mark 7:3).

Breaking bread together, even today, seems to say, We are friends; we share a common bond. Such feelings are apparent throughout the Bible. It is as though eating is more than a matter of ingestion of food; it is participating in all that it means to be human and sharing that mutuality with those around us.

A. Breakfast. The morning meal (in some writings referred to as *dinner*) was usually eaten sometime between 9 o'clock and noon. It was a light meal and consisted of bread, fruits, and cheese.

B. Supper. The principal meal of the day was eaten in the evening. The hot temperatures of the daytime hours in Palestine were somewhat cooled by evening and a more relaxed atmosphere prevailed. Meat, vegetables, butter, and wine were consumed at the evening meal.

C. Feasts. The Jewish people enjoyed celebrations and, according to Scripture, a feast seemed to be a good way to commemorate a joyous event. Music was very much a part of their feasts (Isa. 5:12) and dancing was sometimes a part of the entertainment (as when Herodias' daughter danced for Herod and his guests, Mark 6:32).

The feast was planned and presided over by the "steward" or "governor" of the feast (John 2:8), who directed the servants and tested the food and wine.

Religious festivals, of which feasting was very much a part, may be grouped as follows: (1) The Sabbath, the feast of new moons, the sabbatical year, and the Year of Jubilee; (2) the Passover, Pentecost, and the Feast of Tabernacles; (3) the feasts of Purim and of the dedication. All labor ceased on the principal feast days; the seven-day Passover celebration called for no work on the first and seventh days (Lev. 23).

Feasts were held for marriages (John 2:1-11), on birthdays

(Gen. 40:20), at burials (Jer. 16:7-8), at sheep-shearings (1 Sam. 25:2, 36), and on many other occasions. Possibly the one which comes to mind most frequently is the feast prepared by the father of the prodigal son (Luke 15:11-32).

It is interesting to note that women were never present at Jewish meals as guests.

D. Hospitality. Abraham "sat in the tent door in the heat of the day . . . and behold, three men stood in front by him" (Gen. 18:1-2). Abraham gave them water to drink and to wash the dust from their feet. They sat in the shade of his tree and he and Sarah prepared food for them to eat. His guests turned out to be angels!

In Hebrews 13:2 we are entreated, "Be not forgetful to entertain strangers: for thereby some have entertained angels unawares." Hospitality, kindness to strangers, and "especially unto them who are of the household of faith" (Gal. 6:10), had roots in the Old Testament and became an integral part of the teachings of the New Testament.

E. Table. In ancient Palestine the only table was a circular skin or piece of leather placed on the floor mat. Around the edges of this tray-like table were loops through which a cord was drawn. When the meal was finished, the cord was tightened and the "table" was hung out of the way.

In later times a regular table with reclining couches was introduced. Guests leaned on the table with their left elbow and ate with their right hand.

F. Utensils. Various vessels were probably represented by the use of this word. Sacred vessels referred to in Exodus 25:29 include plates, flagons, and bowls. An ordinary dish used in a household comes to mind in 2 Kings 21:13: "I will wipe Jerusalem as a man wipeth a dish, wiping it, and turning it upside down."

G. The Sop. Table utensils were not used among the Hebrews. The *sop* was a piece of bread used to dip in the soup or broth which sat in the center of the table. The master of the feast might dip a sop and give it to a guest. Jesus gave a sop to Judas (John 13:26), indicating that he was the one who was to betray Jesus.

FASTS

Feasting was an important part of Jewish life, but fasting (going without food for a period of time) was just as essential. Fasts were prescribed for the Day of Atonement by the Mosaic Code ("afflict your souls," Lev. 16:29), to commemorate the breaking of the tables of the Law, and for other such events in Jewish history.

Fasting was practiced to show humility, sorrow, and dependence upon God. Garments of sackcloth, ashes sprinkled on one's head, unwashed hands, and an unanointed head were signs that a person was observing a fast.

Though fasting became an act of hypocrisy for some (Matt. 6:16-18), we do have record of Jesus' fasting for 40 days and nights when He was in the wilderness (Matt. 4:2). It appears that it is a matter left mainly to individual choice.

The Law of Moses avowed the use of wine; however, drunkenness was forbidden. Wine was used as the drink-offering of the daily sacrifice (Exod. 29:40). Nazarites were forbidden to drink it (Num. 6:3), as were also the priests when they performed the services of the temple (Lev. 10:9). Paul

Winepress. Troughs like this one in Jerusalem contained grapes from which wine was made. Holding onto overhead ropes, men tramped on the grapes to extract the juice, which flowed from a hole in the bottom of the trough into a vat (cf. Neh. 13:15).

suggests to Timothy that those who are deacons should not be "given to much wine" (1 Tim. 3:8). There seems to be no doubt that excess drinking was a problem then as it continues to be today.

Included in a list of laws and ordinances is the admonition not to "delay to offer the first . . . of thy liquors" (Exod. 22:29). The Hebrew word which the KJV translated as *liquors* seems to have meant the juice of olives and grapes. The "liquor of grapes" mentioned in Numbers 6:3 was a drink made by steeping grapes.

The dregs of wine (lees) were used to improve the flavor, color, and strength of new wine. "Wines on the lees well refined" (Isa. 25:6) referred to a rich full-bodied wine—a symbol of the blessings of the feast of the Lord.

Jesus was offered a drink of vinegar on a sponge as He hung on the cross. This was probably the sour wine which the Roman soldiers drank (Matt. 27:48). Though not a desirable drink, vinegar was used for dipping bread (Ruth 2:14). When poured on nitre, vinegar produces an effervescent effect. Thus: "As vinegar upon nitre, so is he that singeth songs to an heavy heart" (Prov. 25:20).

GRAIN

A generous supply of grain seems to indicate a well-fed people. Think of the importance placed on Joseph's task of storing the extra grain during the seven years of plenty in Egypt (Gen. 41:47-57). "All countries came into Egypt to Joseph for to buy corn" (v. 57). Grain makes bread—and bread can sustain nations.

A. Barley. Barley was cultivated in Palestine and Egypt and was fed to cattle and horses. Though the Egyptians used barley to feed animals, the Hebrews used it for bread, at least for the poor.

B. Corn. The KJV's references to *corn* (such as Deut. 23:25 and Matt. 12:1) actually mean various kinds of grain, including barley, millet, and wheat. Corn as we know it was not cultivated in the Eastern Hemisphere. Boaz gave Ruth "parched corn" (Ruth 2:14), grain that had been roasted.

C. Millet. Mentioned in Ezekiel 4:9 among other grains, millet is a maize-like grass grown in Palestine and used for bread. It is also used as seeds for birds in Europe.

D. Rye. Though rye ("rie") is mentioned in Exodus 9:32, rye was actually never cultivated in Palestine. Authorities believe that the reference signifies another grain such as millet or spelt.

E. Wheat. "A corn of wheat . . . if it die . . . bringeth forth much fruit" (John 12:24). Jesus speaks here of one of the most widely used of all grains among the Hebrews. Referred to throughout the Bible as a staple of the Hebrew diet, wheat is one of the plants which Moses promised could be grown in Canaan, the Promised Land (Deut. 8:8).

F. The Mill. The simplest kind of mill used to grind grain into meal was called a *mortar*—a hollowed-out stone that held

Flour mill. Hand mills for grinding grain into flour consisted of two circular stones, the lower having a slightly convex surface to guide the drifting bit of broken grain toward the outer edge, where they dropped off. The millstones had curved furrows that multiplied their cutting and grinding effect as the upper stone was rotated on the lower. Larger grain mills were operated by donkeys or slaves. These Roman flour mills from Pompeii are of the larger type. Notice the bread oven behind them.

grain to be pounded by another stone. A more efficient mill consisted of two stones, 60 cm. (2 ft.) in diameter and 15 cm. (6 in.) thick. The *nether* (or lower) *stone* was raised in the center. The upper stone was hollowed out and had a hole in the middle. Grain was poured into the hole, and the upper stone was turned by means of a handle. The grain was crushed as it fell between the two stones. To get very fine flour, the grain had to be ground more than once.

The millstone was so important to the Hebrew people that the Law stated that "no man shall take the . . . millstone to pledge," for he would be taking a man's life in pledge (Deut. 24:6).

G. The Sieve. After the meal was sifted in a sieve, what remained would be returned to the millstone to be ground again. Ancient sieves were made of rushes and papyrus. Isaiah speaks of the nations being sifted with the sieve of vanity (Isa. 30:28).

BREAD

"Give us this day our daily bread" (Matt. 6:11). Jesus prayed for bread, meaning food in general. But bread itself was a staple of Hebrew diet. Grain—usually wheat, but also barley—was milled, sifted, made into a dough, kneaded, formed into thin cakes, and then baked.

Expressions like "bread of sorrows" (Psa. 127:2) and "bread of wickedness" (Prov. 4:17) may indicate that these experiences become as much a part of life as daily bread is a part of life.

A. Showbread. Each Sabbath 12 loaves of unleavened bread (for the 12 tribes of Israel) were baked. They were placed in two piles or rows on the golden table in the sanctuary as an offering to the Lord. When the old bread was removed, it could be eaten only by the priests in the court of the sanctuary (Lev. 24:5-9).

B. Leaven. Jesus uses the term *leaven* (a ferment used in bread to make it rise) in a figurative sense, as He does many well-known everyday terms. In Matthew 13:33 He likens the kingdom to leaven, with its power to change the whole.

Perhaps we are most familiar with this term when we use it in connection with unleavened bread. Bread without leavening was used at times in peace offerings and also during the week of the Passover to remind the Israelites of their release from Egyptian bondage.

C. Wafer. This thin unleavened cake made of wheat flour and anointed with oil was used in offerings (Exod. 16:31; Num. 6:15).

D. Cracknels. These hard biscuits or crumbcakes are mentioned in 1 Kings 14:3. They are called *cracknels* in the KJV because they made a cracking noise when they were broken.

BAKING

Baking was usually done by women. The hearth was frequently used; but at times a thin dough was formed on a heated stone pitcher and then baked. Typically, dough made of wheat or barley was kneaded in a wooden bowl, made into circular cakes, pricked, and baked around a jar or in a bowl. Fresh bread was baked every day. Public bakers are referred to in Hosea 7:4, 6.

A. The Oven. The ovens of the Hebrews were probably of three kinds: (1) The sand oven, in which a fire was built on clean sand and then removed when the sand was hot. Dough was spread on the hot sand in thin layers to bake. (2) The earth oven, the "range for pots" (Lev. 11:35), was a hole in the earth in which stones were heated. Dough was spread in thin layers on the stones after the fire had been removed. (3) Portable ovens, referred to in "baked in the oven" (Lev. 2:4) were probably made of clay. Inside them a fire was built. When they were hot, thin layers of dough were spread on the stones lining the bottom of the oven after the ashes had been removed.

B. The Hearth. Abraham told Sarah to "make cakes upon the hearth" (Gen. 18:6). He was referring to hot stones used

Bread pan. This platter from Lachish (*ca.* fifteenth century B.C.) may have been used for forming cakes of bread or for baking them (*cf.* Lev. 2:5).

for baking bread. The hearth could also mean the fuel that burnt on it (Psa. 102:3) or a portable furnace (Jer. 36:22-23).

MEAT AND RELATED FOODS

The eating of meat is mentioned in the covenant God made with Noah: "Every moving thing that liveth shall be meat for you" (Gen. 9:3). Though the Hebrews' normal diet consisted of vegetables and fruits, they did eat some meat, particularly for banquets and feasts. The early church had a disagreement concerning eating meat offered to idols, but Paul made it clear that nothing is unclean to those who are pure (Titus 1:15; cf. 1 Tim. 4:4).

A. Calf. When the prodigal son returned home, his father killed a fatted calf for a feast (Luke 15:23). In Hebrew life, the calf was considered the choicest of all meats. It was reserved for the most festive occasions.

B. Kid. The prodigal son's older brother became angry and said to his father, "Thou never gavest me a kid, that I might make merry with my friends" (Luke 15:29). The kid (a young goat) was the more common meat, cheaper, and eaten by the poor. It was used in sacrificial offerings (Num. 7:11-87).

C. Fowl. Some fowl were considered unclean for food (Deut. 14:20). But partridge, quail, geese, and pigeons might be eaten.

D. Fish. A favorite food in Palestine was fish, caught in large quantities from the Sea of Galilee and the Jordan River.

After His resurrection, Jesus prepared a breakfast of fish and bread on a charcoal fire by the seashore for some of the disciples (John 21:9-13). Another time when He appeared to the disciples after the Resurrection He asked for something to eat. Luke tells us, "They gave him a piece of broiled fish, . . . and he took it and did eat before them" (Luke 24:42-43).

The Law stated that all fish with fins and scales were clean and therefore could be eaten (Deut. 14:9-10).

E. Sheep (Lamb). Besides its many uses other than food, the sheep was important for its meat, milk, and the fat in its tail, which sometimes weighed as much as fifteen pounds. At the Passover celebration a lamb was killed and eaten to recall the freedom from slavery in Egypt.

F. Fat. The pure fat from an animal was sacrificed to God, since it was considered the richest or best part (Lev. 3:16). It could not be eaten in early times, but this stipulation seemed to be ignored when animals were killed to be used only for food (Deut. 12:15).

HUNTING

Lions, bears, jackals, foxes, hart, roebucks, and fallow-deer are mentioned in the Old Testament. Some of these animals were hunted for food, being caught by a pitfall, a trap, or a net. Isaac instructed Esau to take his bow and quiver and hunt game so that he could have the food he loved (Gen. 27:3-4). The blood of these wild animals was not eaten.

Though not used as utensils for eating as we know them, knives were necessary for killing animals and in preparing them for eating or for sacrifice (Lev. 8:20; Ezra 1:9).

COOKING

Cooking was woman's work, particularly in the years before the conquest of Canaan. For roasting, a wood fire was built or an oven was used. For boiling, the animal was cut up, put in a kettle (cauldron) with water, and seasoned (Ezek. 24:4-5). The meat and broth were served separately. Vegetables were also boiled.

A cauldron was a large metal vessel used for boiling meat (1 Sam. 2:14). A 3-pronged fork was used for removing meat from the cauldron.

MILK PRODUCTS

"A land flowing with milk and honey" was promised to the Israelites (Josh. 5:6), and in that promise they envisioned abundance and prosperity. The Hebrews drank the milk of camels, sheep, and goats. The camel's milk was especially rich and strong, but not very sweet. References to milk are found throughout the Old Testament (cf. Prov. 27:27; Deut. 32:14).

A. Butter. The Hebrew term *chemah* has been variously translated as *cream, curds, cheese,* and *butter.* According to Genesis 18:8, Abraham served butter *(chemah)* to the strangers who visited his tent. Proverbs 30:33 tells us that "the churning of milk bringeth forth butter." Whatever the exact meaning of the Hebrew word, there is some agreement that the Hebrews did use a kind of butter. It was probably made in the same manner that the Arabs use today. Heated milk, to which a small amount of sour milk *(leben)* is added, is poured into a goatskin bag and shaken until the butter separates. It is drained and after 3 days is heated again. Butter thus prepared keeps well in the hot climate of Palestine.

B. Cheese. With cheese, we have somewhat the same problem as we have with butter; it is difficult to know for sure what the writers meant. Consider: "Didst thou not . . . curdle me like cheese?" (Job 10:10, RSV); "Take these ten cheeses unto the captain" (1 Sam. 17:18); ". . . honey and butter, and sheep, and cheese of kine . . . to eat" (2 Sam. 17:29). In each of these references, the word for *cheese* in the original is a different word. It is likely that cheese in these three instances means a coagulated milk.

FRUIT

A favorite food of the Hebrews was the fruit which grew in abundance in the warm climate of that part of the world. The spies whom Moses sent to Canaan brought back a branch bearing a single cluster of grapes which was so large that they carried it on a pole between them. They also brought back pomegranates and figs (Num. 13:23). These and a variety of other fruits were enjoyed as a part of the regular diet.

A. Grapes. See the section on "Wine," above.

B. Raisins. "Bunches of raisins" were brought to David "for there was joy in Israel" (1 Chron. 12:40). Raisins were grapes that were dried in bunches. They are also mentioned in 1 Samuel 25:18 and 2 Samuel 16:1.

C. Flagon. Though *flagon* in Isaiah 22:24 surely means a kind of vessel, another usage of the word in 2 Samuel 6:19 means "a cake of raisins." It comes from the Hebrew *'ashishah* ("pressed together"). Flagons appear to be dried grapes or raisins that are pressed into a cake. They were used as a sacrifice to idols (Hos. 3:1) and were enjoyed as a delicacy.

D. Pomegranate. This beautiful rose-red fruit with its many seeds was a favorite among the Israelites. The abundance of seeds was symbolic of fertility and it was grown both for its tasty fruit and for its beauty in the garden. The juice of the pomegranate was highly prized (Sol. 8:2). It was one of the fruits which were grown in the Promised Land (Num. 13:23).

The robe of the high priest was decorated with ornamental

"pomegranates of blue, and of purple, and of scarlet, round about the hem thereof" (Exod. 28:33). Two hundred ornamental pomegranates decorated each of the two free-standing pillars (Jachin and Boaz) in Solomon's temple (2 Chron. 3:13).

E. Melon. The Israelites were camped in the hot Arabian Desert with only manna to eat. They complained in the Lord's hearing, "We remember . . . the melons" in Egypt (Num. 11:5). This is the only reference to melons in the Bible. It is impossible to tell whether they meant the muskmelon or the watermelon, or both, since it is possible that both grew in Egypt at that time. Whatever the case, the melon was a refreshing treat when the weather was hot.

F. Apple. The apple or apple tree mentioned in the KJV is probably the citron tree and fruit, although the quince and apricot have also been suggested. From the Bible we learn that the fruit of this "apple tree" is sweet (Song of Sol. 2:3); its fruit is gold in color (Prov. 25:11); and it is fragrant (Song of Sol. 7:8).

"A word fitly spoken is like apples of gold in pictures of silver" (Prov. 25:11). Literally: "A word fitly spoken is like golden citrons in silver baskets."

G. Fig. From the fig leaves used by Adam and Eve as coverings for their nakedness (Gen. 3:7) to the fig tree that Jesus cursed (Mark 11:4), figs are mentioned throughout the Bible. They were a common fruit in Palestine. Fig trees grow singly or in small groups and provide a delightful shade with their large leaves (cf. John 1:48). They are eaten fresh from the tree, dried, or pressed into cakes (1 Sam. 25:18).

H. Olive. "And the dove came in to him in the evening; . . . in her mouth was an olive leaf plucked off" (Gen. 8:11). Noah received the symbol of peace and plenty and knew that the waters had gone down. The olive, a common fruit in Palestine, resembles a plum and is first green, then pale in color, and finally black when fully ripe. The tree itself resembles an apple tree and will bear fruit even when very old. The clusters of flowers when the tree is in bloom remind one of lilac.

Olives are beaten or shaken from the tree and some fruit was to be left for the poor (Deut. 24:20). The fruit was eaten—

both green and ripe—but the largest portion of the olive harvest was squeezed for oil.

The best oil comes from the green fruit. It is referred to in Exodus 27:20 as "pure olive oil beaten." The first extraction, shaken in pans or baskets, produces the finest oil; the second and third extractions are inferior. Oil was used for anointing, with food and cooking, and for lamps. A good tree will produce 60 lit. (12 gal.) of oil a year.

Oil was extracted from the olives in heavy stone oil presses called *gath-shemen* (Gethsemane is derived from this word; Matt. 26:36). Micah 6:15 speaks of treading the oil from the olives, as with grapes. Other references suggest that a large millstone was laid on its flat surface and was depressed on the upper surface. Another stone was placed upright on top of this and a beam was passed through its center. A horse or ox or man turned the top stone and the oil was pressed out by the weight.

The "oil-tree" mentioned in Isaiah 41:19 is surely the olive tree. One authority suggests that this refers to the oleaster, a shrub that yields an inferior oil. But general agreement speaks in favor of the olive.

VEGETABLES

"Let them give us pulse [vegetables] to eat, and water to drink" (Dan. 1:12). Daniel requested the simple food of his people rather than the king's rich diet. "And at the end of ten days their countenances appeared fairer and fatter in flesh than all the children which did eat the portion of the king's meat (v. 15).

Vegetables were everyday fare for the Israelites. Vegetable gardens are mentioned in Deuteronomy 11:10 and 1 Kings 21:2.

A. Bean. Beans along with other foods were brought to David as he was fleeing from Absalom (2 Sam. 17:28). Again, in Ezekiel 4:9, a bread made of wheat, barley, lentils, millet, and fitches, with beans, is described. A porridge was made by adding pounded beans to wheat meal or to bruised wheat. Garden beans flavored with oil and garlic were boiled and enjoyed.

B. Lentil. Esau sold his birthright for a bowl of pottage made from red lentils (Gen. 25:29-34). Lentils are similar to garden peas and the red lentils are considered to be the best. As with beans, lentils are sometimes used by the poor to make bread.

C. Cucumber. It is commonly agreed that *cucumber* is a proper translation of the Hebrew words *shakaph* and *miqshah* (Num. 11:5; Isa. 1:8). Two types of cucumber were grown in Bible times—the long adder, ready for harvest in July, and the gherkin, which is marketed into September.

The Hebrews longed for the cucumbers along with the melons of Egypt when they had nothing but manna to eat in the wilderness (Num. 11:5). An interesting custom among the Hebrews was to build leafy watch places for a guard to sit in and watch for thieves. When the crop season was over, they were abandoned. In Isaiah 1:8, we are told that Zion was "left as . . . a lodge in a garden of cucumbers"—desolate.

Assyrian banquet. Attended by servants and musicians, King Ashurbanipal and his queen feast in their garden in this relief from his palace (*ca.* sixth century B.C.). Like the Assyrians, the ancient Hebrews frequently celebrated religious and social occasions with feasts, accompanied by music and dancing.

D. Onion and Garlic. These two flavorful bulb-like vegetables grow well in hot countries. Onions and garlic were a part of the memory of the good things of Egypt when the Israelites became fretful in the desert. The reference to these roots in Numbers 11:5 beyond a doubt means the onion and garlic with which we are familiar. Sheep and camels have been known to thrive on them.

E. Leek. The word *leeks* appears only one time in the KJV Bible (Num. 11:5). The same original word appears several times, but in all other cases is translated differently. Various opinions identify them as any green vegetable food, such as a vegetable eaten with bread by the poor and made into a meat sauce by the rich, as is today's leek. It is probably a kind of lotus, the root of which was boiled and eaten as a condiment.

F. Pottage. Jacob's pottage is famous (Gen. 25:29-34). Pottage was a soup made of lentils and seasoned with oil and garlic.

Another interesting story about pottage is told in 2 Kings 4:38-41. Other ingredients were used in this type of pottage.

G. Bitter Herbs. This salad-like dish was a part of the Passover feast. It was used to remind the Hebrews of the sorrow they experienced in Egypt before they were free (Exod. 12:8; Num. 9:11). Greens included in the herbs could have been horseradish, lettuce, endive, parsley, and watercress.

NUTS

Jacob sent nuts as a gift to Joseph in Egypt (Gen. 43:11). Nuts probably did not grow in that country. A nut orchard is spoken of in Song of Solomon 6:11.

A. Almond. This early-blooming tree is called *shaked* in the Hebrew language, which means "watch, vigilant." Because of its early flowering, the symbol of the almond is used in Ecclesiastes 12:5 to represent the rapid aging of mankind. Jeremiah also uses the almond to express God's swift performance of His word (Jer. 1:11-12).

Aaron's rod budded, blossomed, and bore almonds in the tabernacle. Through this miracle the people understood that the house of Levi, represented by Aaron was declared to be the priestly tribe (Num. 17:1-9).

There are two types of almonds. The bitter almond is known for its oil; the sweet almond is used for desserts.

B. Pistachio. The RSV says that Jacob also sent pistachio nuts to Joseph in Egypt (Gen. 43:11). This is the only time they are mentioned in the Bible. They were used in confections.

HONEY

The law of the Lord is "sweeter . . . than honey and the honeycomb" (Psa. 19:10). References to this delicacy run throughout the Bible from Genesis to Revelation. The Israel-

Arabs eating. Breaking bread together was the primary expression of hospitality in the ancient Near East, as it is today. Some scholars believe that the Hebrews ate twice a day—a light meal in the morning and a heavier meal in the cool evening. In earlier times, meals were served on floor mats, as shown here. Couches were used in the Roman era.

ites were led to a "land flowing with milk and honey" (Exod. 3:8); at least 20 references in the Bible are worded similarly. Honey could not be offered on the altar of the Lord (Lev. 2:11), possibly because certain heathen nations practiced such a custom.

Jeroboam, when his child became ill, sent his wife to the prophet Ahijah with "a cruse of honey" (1 Kings 14:3). John the Baptist's "meat was locusts and wild honey" (Matt. 3:4).

The word *honey* in some references may mean the syrup of dates or grapes (Hebrew, *dibs*). The phrase "suck honey out of the rock" (Deut. 32:13) comes from the fact that bees sometimes deposit their honey on the rocks and cover it with a wax.

MANNA

The children of Israel, after they left Egypt, came to the wilderness of Sin, which is between Elim and Sinai. They began to complain to Moses and Aaron: "Would to God we had died . . . in the land of Egypt . . . ; ye have brought us forth . . . to kill [us] with hunger." The Lord heard their complaining and He said, "I will rain bread from heaven for you; and the people shall go out and gather a certain rate every day." On the sixth day, they were to gather an extra day's portion for the Sabbath. *Manna* did not fall on the Sabbath. The Lord continued to provide the miraculous bread every morning except the Sabbath for forty years, until the Israelites entered the land of Canaan (Exod. 16).

Some authorities attempt to give natural explanations for the manna, the most common of which has to do with the tamarisk tree. This tree presently is found in the peninsula of Sinai. A saccharine-like sap drips from this tree during certain seasons of the year and resembles the description of the manna supplied to the Israelites. Exodus 16:14 says it was "a small round thing, as small as the hoar frost on the ground" (v. 14). "It was like coriander seed, white, and the taste of it was like wafers made with honey" (Exod. 16:31).

Some authorities are convinced that tamarisk sap is the

The Traditional Passover

The Passover ritual stands at the center of Jewish worship. Every element of *Pesach* (Hebrew, "Passover") was designed to commemorate the Jews' historic passage from slavery to nationhood under God.

Passover is a seven-day celebration in which the main feast occurs the first night. The *seder* (Hebrew, "service") meal with its accompanying ritual recalls the last meal the Jews ate in Egypt before beginning their journey to the Promised Land. Jews are commanded to remember their history of captivity and liberation on the night of the Seder: "And thou shalt show thy son in that day, saying, This is done because of that which the Lord did unto me when I came forth out of Egypt" (Exod. 13:8).

Of the many traditional ingredients of the Seder table, the most important are those which God specified for the last meal in Egypt: "Your lamb shall be without blemish, a male a year old" (Exod. 12:5). The lambs must be roasted, not boiled. Seder participants are reminded that lamb's blood was smeared on the doorposts of Jewish houses to protect Jews from the plague that struck nonbelievers the first Passover night.

The paschal lamb was to be eaten with bitter herbs, as commanded in Exodus. In Old Testament times bitter lettuce, chicory, or endive were used; today Jewish families are more likely to use grated horseradish or onion. These herbs symbolize the bitterness of captivity under the Egyptians.

Since the first Seder was eaten as Jews prepared for flight, the theme of haste is woven into the feast. Unleavened bread of a cracker-like texture, such as *matzos,* was more suitable for a people in flight than leavened loaves, which required kneading and rising.

Each participant in the Seder has a wine cup. The host of the feast leans on cushions, recalling the ancient mode of eating in a reclining position. In front of the host is placed the Seder plate, with the traditional symbolic foods: three wafers of matzo bread wrapped in a napkin, the bitter herbs, the *haroset* or fruit pulp, the roasted lamb and hardboiled egg, the sweet vegetables, and a dish of salt water for washing hands.

The best-known part of the Seder ritual is probably the "Four Questions." The youngest male child of the house asks questions about the Seder, beginning with the words, "Why is this night of Passover different from all other nights of the year?" He asks about the use of unleavened bread, bitter herbs, the dipping of vegetables, and the cushions at the host's chair. The host answers the child by reciting the history of Israel's passage from bondage to freedom.

While the preparation for the Seder requires a great deal of patience, none of the traditional foods presents any difficulties. The *haroset* is the only one that requires any special recipe, and there are many versions available. In fact, the important thing about the *haroset* is its texture (which resembles mortar) rather than its ingredients. A simple haroset might include grated apples, chopped nuts, sugar, cinnamon, and sweet red wine. These ingredients are mashed together to the consistency of a dip. Matzo meal can be added, other fruits or nuts substituted, and the sugar and cinnamon added to the individual taste.

---

same as the original manna. Others contradict this conclusion for the following reasons: (1) The original manna lasted 40 years continuously; the tamarisk manna is unpredictable and seasonal. (2) The quantity produced by the tamarisk manna would not begin to feed three to four million people daily. (3) The original manna fell from heaven; the tamarisk manna fell from twigs on the tree. (4) The original manna could not be kept for more than a day; the tamarisk manna lasts for months. (5) The original manna could be boiled, ground, pounded, and made into cakes; the tamarisk manna could not be so used. (6) The nutrients were different—the original sustained a nation for 40 years; the tamarisk was only saccharine matter.

Hospitality. God told the Israelites to be hospitable (Lev. 19:34). This meant that they should offer food, shelter, and clothing to travelers passing through their lands. An important Hebrew custom was the washing of the guests' feet, a gesture of welcome in a hot, dusty country where stony roads often made foot travel a painful experience.

8

CLOTHING AND COSMETICS

The Israelites' manner of dress changed gradually over the centuries. Let us note how 5 basic articles of clothing evolved.

God made garments for Adam and Eve. "Unto Adam also and to his wife did the Lord God make coats of skins, and clothed them" (Gen. 3:21). This garment (Hebrew, *kethon*) was a simple shirt made of animal skin. Later, the Hebrews began making shirts from linen or silk (if the garment was to be worn by an important individual). Thus, we read that Joseph wore the "coat of many colors" (Gen. 37:3), which the RSV renders as a "long robe with sleeves."

While the *kethon* remained the costume of the common people, another form of dress called the *simlah* came into fashion. Shem and Japheth took this garment to cover the nakedness of their father (Gen. 9:23). At first, the Israelites made the *simlah* of wool, but later camel's hair was used. It was an outer garment resembling a large sheet with a hood, and the Jews used it for additional warmth. The poor used it for their basic dress by day and for cover by night (Exod. 22:26-27).

The Israelites wore the *beged* for special occasions indoors. Isaac and Rebekah dressed their son Jacob in this garment, which they considered their best clothing (Gen. 27:15). The Israelites thought the *beged* a badge of dignity to the wearer, and it was worn by distinguished members of great families. After the temple rituals were instituted, priests wore the *beged*.

The fourth item of clothing, the *lebhosh* (meaning "to clothe"), was a garment used for general wear. However, it eventually became an outer garment for both the rich and the poor. Thus, the Bible says that Mordecai wore a *lebhosh* of sackcloth (Esther 4:2), while a more exquisite *lebhosh* could serve as "royal apparel" (Esther 8:15). The Psalmist referred to this garment when he wrote, "They part my garments amongst them, and cast lots upon vesture" (Psa. 22:15).

Finally, the *addereth* was worn to indicate that the wearer was a person of importance (Josh. 7:21). This garment was also a type of cloak or outer covering. By contrast, such a cloak is worn by various people in Palestine today, regardless of their station in life.

These examples demonstrate how the use of certain garments changed as Jewish society changed. And the manufacture of these garments points to the availability of different textile materials in each era of history.

This article will discuss 4 different aspects of the clothing of Bible times—fabrics, men's clothing, women's clothing, and priests' clothing. We will also note how Near Eastern people used cosmetics and jewelry.

TYPES OF FABRICS

Genesis 3:7 tells how Adam and Eve realized they were naked and sewed fig leaves together to make "aprons" (Hebrew, *hagor*). Then the Creator made Adam and Eve shirts of skins, as we saw, before sending them out of the Garden of Eden (Gen. 3:21). Later, various fabrics were used to make clothes.

A. Linen. Linen was one of the most important fabrics for the Israelites. It was made from the flax plant, which was cultivated especially for that purpose. The Canaanites grew flax in Palestine before the Israelites conquered that country (Josh. 2:6).

Linen was a versatile fabric that could be made coarse and thick, or very fine and delicate. The Egyptians had a wide reputation for their fine linen, which was nearly transparent. They also made coarse linen that was so heavy that it could be used for carpets to cover the floors.

The fine linen fabrics were worn by those with positions of status or wealth (cf. Luke 16:19), and the coarser fabrics were worn by the common people. The Egyptians clothed Joseph in fine linen when they made him ruler (Gen. 41:42).

The curtains, veil, and door hangings of the Hebrew tabernacle were made of fine linen (Exodus 26:1, 31, 36), as were the hangings for the gate of the court and for the court itself (Exod. 27:9, 16, 18). The ephod and breastpiece of the high priest contained fine linen (Exod. 28:6, 15). The tunic, girdle, and breeches worn by all priests were also made of fine white linen (Exod. 28:39; 39:27-28).

The Jews made their inner garments, or underclothing, primarily of linen. The graveclothes of Jesus were made from this fabric. Scripture says that Joseph of Arimathea "bought fine linen, and took him down, and wrapped him in the linen" (Mark 15:46). Fine white linen was also a symbol of innocence and moral purity (Rev. 15:6).

B. Wool. The Jews used sheep's wool as the principal material for making clothes. The merchants of Damascus in Syria found a ready market for their fine wool in the port city of Tyre (Ezek. 27:15). Wool is one of the oldest materials used for woven cloth.

God's Law did not allow the Israelites to weave garments from a mixture of wool and linen (Deut. 22:11). This law resembled several other precepts—such as not sowing mingled seed in a field, or not ploughing with an ox and an ass together (Lev. 17:19-25). Perhaps these laws symbolically expressed the idea of separateness and simplicity that characterized the ancient people of God. On the other hand, the vestments of the high priest were made of such a mixture. Therefore, the mixture may have been considered holy and inappropriate for common apparel.

Wool remained one of the chief materials for dress. Indeed, the economy of Bible lands relied heavily upon wool.

C. Silk. Ezekiel 16:10, 13 describes silk as a fabric of great value. The Hebrew words for this cloth were *sheshî* and *meshî*. Some scholars think the term found in Proverbs 31:22 (*sheshî*) actually refers to fine linen. We do not know if the Egyptians used silk, but the Chinese and other Asiatics used it in Old Testament times. Silk certainly reached the Bible lands after

Clothing and Climate

Climate is a primary factor in determining a people's style of dress. This can be seen by comparing the dress of ancient Hebrews with the dress of peoples who lived in different climate zones.

Egyptians of the Nile Valley shaved their heads and bodies to keep cool and clean, and developed linen cloth—virtually the lightest of clothing materials—to offset the effects of the sweltering sun in their area. Egyptian workers wore a simple loincloth; in primitive times, this was also accepted garb for men in general. By the time of King Tutankhamen (fourteenth century B.C.), the loincloth had developed into a longer garment, much like an apron. Light cloaks or capes were worn over the shoulder. Women wore a long, loose garment that reached from below the arms to the ankle, and was held in place over the shoulders by one or two straps. The only sleeved garment of the Egyptians was the *kalasiris*, a rectangle of linen cloth with separate sleeves sewn in.

The Egyptians preferred the sheerest of linens. For shoes they wore leather or rush sandals. Headgear consisted of conical hats for men and headbands for women. Many Egyptians carried fans, which served a useful purpose in the hot region, in addition to being decorative.

Contrast the dress of ancient Egyptians with that of the Celts, a barbarian people who lived north of the Alps by at least the sixth century B.C. The Celts were tall, muscular, light-skinned people who lived and worked in a harsh, cold climate. Their basic economy was farming. They raised cattle, cultivated cereal, and engaged in other types of farming—all in climates considerably colder than that of Egypt.

The Celts might wear thick undergarments and a type of stocking or legging, depending on the weather in their region. Men of the Cisalpine tribes wore trousers by the third century B.C. By that time, the Celts also preferred to wear belted tunics or shirts with a cloak. They wrapped cloth about their feet. Celtic women wore a single long garment with a cloak.

The Celts preferred coarse linens and wool for protection against the cold. Their clothing was colored in a wide spectrum, from the darkest shades to sun hues and whites. The Egyptians, on the other hand, preferred white; their only alternate colors were light blues, yellows, and greens.

These extremes in clothing styles—from linen loincloths in Egypt to coarse shirts in northern Europe—points up the role that climate plays in determining the type of garments that different peoples prefer.

---

the conquest of Alexander the Great (*ca.* 325 B.C.). But it may have come to Palestine earlier, since Solomon traded with surrounding countries that might have produced this fabric.

The fineness and vivid color of fabrics increased their value, so silk held an important position in the ancient world. The luxury lovers of New Testament "Babylon" (Rome?) treasured silk (Rev. 18:12). As late as A.D. 275, unmixed silk goods were sold for their weight in gold.

D. Sackcloth. The Israelites used sackcloth as a ritual sign of repentance or a token of mourning. The dark color and coarse texture of this goat's hair material made it ideal for that use. When Joseph's brothers sold him to the Ishmaelites, Jacob put on sackcloth to mourn the loss of his son (Gen. 37:24). In times of extreme sorrow, the Israelites wore this rough material next to their skin, as Job did (Job 16:15).

The New Testament also associated sackcloth with repentance, as we find in Matthew 11:21: "For if the mighty works which were done in you, had been done in Tyre and Sidon, they would have repented long ago in sackcloth and ashes." The sorrowful Israelite would clothe himself in sackcloth, place ashes upon his head, and then sit in the ashes. Our modern Western custom of wearing dark colors to funerals corresponds to the Israelites' gesture of wearing sackcloth.

Sackcloth material was also used to make grain sacks (Gen. 42:25; Josh. 9:4).

E. Cotton. We do not know whether the Israelites used cotton for making clothes. The Hebrew *pishtah* meant a type of material from plants, as opposed to animal material such as wool. The term could refer to the flax plant (as per the RSV) from which linen was made, or possibly to the cotton bush (as per the KJV).

Although the Hebrew word *karpas* was usually translated as if it meant a color (Esther 1:6; 8:15), it may possibly refer to cotton. Both Syria and Palestine grow cotton today; but we are not sure whether the Hebrews knew of cotton before they came into contact with Persia.

MANUFACTURE OF FABRICS

Jewish women made clothes out of necessity. The preparation of fabrics and the actual making of clothes were considered to be women's duties. Several processes were involved.

A. Distaff Spinning. Jewish women used distaff spinning to make cloth, since the spinning wheel was unknown at that time. They would attach wool or flax to the *distaff* (a rod or stick), and then use a *spindle* to twist the fibers into threads. The Bible mentions this art in Exodus 35:25-26 and Proverbs 31:19.

B. Weaving. After the women spun the raw materials into thread, they used the thread to weave cloth. We call the lengthwise threads the *warp* and the cross threads the *woof.* The women would attach the woof to a *shuttle,* an instrument that held the thread so that it could be passed over and under the threads of the warp. Scripture does not specifically describe the use of a shuttle, but it is implied in Job 7:6. The warp was attached to a wooden beam at the top or the bottom of the loom, and the weaver stood while working. (The Bible does not mention the loom, only the beam to which the warp was attached—Judg. 16:14.) Various textures of fabric could be produced by this method.

The Israelites were probably acquainted with weaving long before their time of slavery in Egypt. But in Egypt they perfected the art to such a degree that they were able to make the temple hangings mentioned in Exodus 35:35.

The Israelites made various kinds of woven fabrics in their years of wandering in the wilderness. These included woolen garments (Lev. 13:48), twined linen (Exod. 26:1), and the embroidered clothing of the priests (Exod. 28:4, 39).

C. Tanning. Tanning was a process that the people of Bible times used to dry animal skins, preparing them to wear. They used lime, the juice of certain plants, and the leaves or bark of certain trees to tan the skins.

Jews considered the tanner's trade disreputable. Peter defied this prejudice by stopping with Simon, a tanner, at Joppa (Acts 9:43). Jewish tanners were usually forced to conduct their business outside town.

D. Embroidering. The Hebrews did beautiful needlework. The term *embroider* (Hebrew *shâbâts* and *râqam*) appears in Exodus 28:39; 35:35; 38:23. The "cunning work" (Hebrew, *châshab*) mentioned in Exodus 26:1 may have been more like embroidery than needlework. However, neither would exactly fit our modern idea of embroidery.

The embroiderer wove cloth with a variety of colors and then sewed a pattern onto it. Thus the decorated part of the cloth was on one side of the fabric. In contrast, the "cunning work" was done by weaving gold thread or figures right into the fabric. The Jews did this sophisticated type of embroidery only on the garments worn by the priests.

E. Dyeing. The Israelites were very familiar with the art of dyeing at the time of their Exodus from Egypt (cf. Exod. 26:1, 14; 35:25). The process of dyeing is described in detail on Egyptian monuments; however, Scripture gives us no precise record of how the Hebrews dyed their cloth.

Undyed cotton and linen were used, with some exceptions. Cotton could be dyed indigo blue, but linen was more difficult to dye. Occasionally blue threads decorated the otherwise plain cloth. When the Bible mentions a fabric color other than blue, it indicates that the fabric was wool.

The natural dye colors used by the Jews were white, black, red, yellow, and green. Red was a very popular color for Hebrew clothing.

The purple dye so famous in the ancient Near East came from a species of shellfish in the Mediterranean Sea. The Hebrews valued purple goods very highly, but they loosely used the term to refer to every color that had a reddish tint.

The New Testament tells us that Lydia was a "seller of purple in the city of Thyatira" (Acts 16:14). Thyatira was famous for its cloth dyers, so we assume that Lydia dealt in cloth of purple and possibly in the dye itself.

CARE OF FABRICS

Clothes were laundered by fullers in Bible times. The English term *fuller* means "one who washes" or "one who treads." The professional fuller would clean garments by stamping on them or beating them with a stick in a tub of water. Jeremiah 2:22 and Malachi 3:2 tell us that nitre and soap were used as cleaning agents. Other substances were also used for cleaning, such as alkali and chalk. To whiten garments, fullers would rub "fuller's earth" (cimolite) into them.

The trade of the fuller created an offensive odor, so it was done outside the city. A place called the "fuller's field" on the northern side of the city of Jerusalem was where fullers washed and dried their clothes. Their water supply came from the upper pool of Gihon on the northern side of the city.

Scripture tells how the king of Assyria sent soldiers against Jerusalem from this northern direction (2 Kings 18:17). It is interesting to note that the fuller's field was so near the city walls that the Assyrian ambassadors standing in the field could be heard on the ramparts.

MEN'S CLOTHING

The Israelites were scarcely influenced by the dress of surrounding countries, since their travel was limited. The fashions of Israelite men remained much the same, generation after generation.

A. General Wear. Ordinarily, Jewish men wore an inner garment, an outer garment, a girdle, and sandals. Modern Arabs use the same flowing robes and make the same distinction between "inner" and "outer" garments—the inner garments being of lightweight material and the outer garments being heavy and warm. Modern Arabs also make a visible distinction between the dress of the rich and poor, the rich wearing much finer materials.

1. Inner Garment. The Israelite man's "inner garment" resembled a close-fitting shirt. The most common Hebrew word for this garment *(kethoneth)* is translated variously as *coat, robe, tunic,* and *garment.* It was made of wool, linen, or cotton. The earliest of these garments were made without sleeves and reached only to the knees. Later, the inner garment extended to the wrists and ankles.

A man wearing only this inner garment was said to be naked (1 Sam. 19:24; Isa. 20:2-4). The New Testament probably refers to this garment when it says Peter "girt his fisher's coat unto him, (for he was naked,) and did cast himself into the sea" (John 21:7).

2. Girdle. The man's girdle was a belt or band of cloth, cord, or leather 10 cm. or more wide. A fastener attached to the girdle allowed it to be loosened or tightened. The Jews used the girdle in two ways: as a tie around the waist of the inner garment or around the outer garment. When used around the inner garment, it was often called the *loincloth* or *waistcloth*. The use of a girdle increased a person's gracefulness of appearance and prevented the long, flowing robes from interfering with daily work and movements.

The biblical expression "to gird up the loins" meant to put on the girdle; it signified that the person was ready for service (1 Pet. 1:13). On the other hand, "to loose the girdle" meant that the person was either lazy or resting (Isa. 5:27).

3. Outer Garment. The Hebrew men wore an "outer garment" consisting of a square or oblong strip of cloth, 2 to 3 m. (80 to 120 in.) wide. This garment *(me'yil)* was called the *coat*, *robe*, or *mantle*. It was wrapped around the body as a protective covering, with two corners of the material being in front. The outer garment was drawn in close to the body by a girdle. Sometimes the Israelites decorated the girdle for this outer garment with rich and beautiful ornaments of metal, precious stones, or embroidery. The poor man used this outer garment as his bed clothing (Exod. 22:26-27). The rich often had a finely woven linen outer garment, and the poor a coarsely woven garment of goat's hair.

Jewish men wore fringes with blue ribbons on the "border" (hemline) of this outer garment (Num. 15:38). The fringes reminded them of the constant presence of the Lord's commandments. Jesus referred to these fringes in Matthew 23:5; apparently, the scribes and Pharisees made these fringes very large so that people could see how faithful they were in doing the Lord's commandments.

The Hebrews often riped the outer garment in times of distress (Ezra 9:3, 5; Job 1:20; 2:12).

A person's number of robes was a measure of wealth in the Near East (cf. James 5:2). Consequently, a large wardrobe indicated that a person was rich and powerful, and a lack of clothing showed poverty. In this connection, note Isaiah 3:6-7.

4. Purse. The man's purse was actually formed by the girdle, which was sewn double and fastened with a buckle. The other end of the girdle was wrapped around the body and then tucked into the first section, which opened and closed with a leather strap. The contents of the purse were placed beneath the strap. Matthew 10:9 and Mark 6:8 refer to this type of purse. Apparently, the Jews also used a type of purse that was separate from the girdle (Luke 10:4).

Jewish men also used a *scrip,* which may have been similar to our modern purse. Shepherds carried their food or other necessities in this type of bag. It seems that the scrip was worn over the shoulder. In such a bag, David carried five stones to slay the giant Goliath (1 Sam. 17:40). The scrip mentioned in the New Testament, carried by shepherds and travelers, might have been made of skins (Mark 6:8).

5. Sandals. The term *sandals* is used only twice in the Bible. In its simplest form, the sandal was a sole of wood fastened with straps of leather (thongs). The disciples of Jesus wore these (Mark 6:9). When an angel appeared to Peter in prison, Peter was told to put on his sandals (Acts 12:8). All classes of people in Palestine wore sandals—even the very poor. In Assyria, sandals also covered the heel and the side of the foot. The sandal and the thong (or "shoe latchet") were so common that they symbolized the most insignificant thing, as in Genesis 14:23.

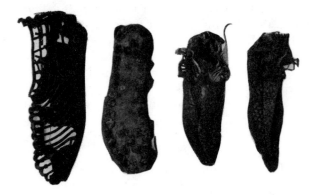

Sandals. Most of the people in ancient lands were barefoot or wore sandals. The poor could not afford shoes, since shoes were made of soft leather, which was scarce. Sandals were of tough leather. Some think the Israelites constructed the soles of wood, cane, or palm bark, nailing them to the leather thongs. Archaeologists have found ancient sandals in great variety. These are from Britain during the time of the Roman occupation; notice the hobnails in the sandal second from left.

Jews did not wear their sandals indoors (Luke 7:38); they removed them upon entering the house, and the feet were washed. Removing the sandals was also a sign of reverence; Moses was told to do it when God spoke to him from the burning bush (Exod. 3:5).

The Jews considered it a very lowly task to carry or to unloose another person's sandals. When John the Baptist spoke of the coming of Christ, he said, "He it is, who coming after me is preferred before me, whose shoe's latchet I am not worthy to unloose" (John 1:27).

Going without sandals was a mark of poverty (Luke 15:22) or a sign of mourning (2 Sam. 13:30; Isa. 20:2-4; Ezek. 24:17, 23).

B. Clothing for Special Occasions. Wealthy Jewish men owned several suits of clothing; each suit consisted of an inner and outer garment. Some of these suits of clothing were made of very thin fabric and were worn over garments of various colors (Isa. 3:22).

1. Robes of Honor. Often a man being installed in a position of honor or importance was given a special robe. Joseph was given such a robe when he was put in a position of leadership in Egypt (Gen. 41:42). On the other hand, the removal of a robe signaled a man's dismissal from office. A fine robe was a mark of a man's special honor in a household (Luke 15:22).

2. Wedding Garments. On grand occasions, a host would give special robes to his guests. At Jewish weddings, for instance, the host furnished wedding garments to all the guests (Matt. 22:11). At times, the wedding party wore crowns (Ezek. 16:12).

3. Mourning Garments. See the section on "Sackcloth" above.

4. Winter Clothing. In the winter, people of the Bible lands wore fur dresses or skins. This type of winter clothing may be indicated in 2 Kings 2:8 and Zechariah 13:4. Common cattle skins were worn by the poorest people (Heb. 11:37), but some fur robes were very costly and were a part of the royal wardrobe.

Sheep's clothing (sheepskin) suggested innocence and gentleness; but Matthew 7:15 speaks of it as a symbol of the disguise of false prophets, who lead the people in the wrong way.

C. Ornaments. Jewish men wore bracelets, rings, chains, and necklaces of various kinds. In the Near East, both sexes wore chains of gold for ornament and dignity. Government officials placed such chains on Joseph and Daniel as symbols of sovereignty (Gen. 41:42; Dan. 5:29). Jewish men had a fondness for improving their personal appearance, and they often used jewelry to do this. The craft of jewelry-making probably developed at a very early period (Num. 31:50; Hos. 2:13).

1. Rings. The Jew used the ring as a seal and token of his authority (Gen. 41:42; Dan. 6:17). With his signet ring he would stamp his personal seal on official documents. It could be worn on a cord around the neck or on the finger. Men also wore rings or bands on the upper arms (cf. 2 Sam. 1:10).

As many as nine rings have been found on a single hand of an Egyptian mummy, indicating that the market for jewelry was quite active. In battles, soldiers took bracelets and anklets from their enemy as part of the spoil. When the Amalekite killed Saul, he brought Saul's bracelet to David as proof of Saul's death (2 Sam. 1:10).

2. Amulets. In the superstitious Near Eastern nations many people feared imaginary spirits. To protect themselves, they wore magical charms. The *amulets* referred to in the Bible were earrings worn by women (Gen. 35:4; Judg. 2:13; 8:24), or pendants suspended from chains around the necks of men. The amulet had sacred words or the figure of a god engraved on it. In another form of amulet, the words were written on a papyrus or parchment scroll that was rolled tightly and sewn up in linen.

3. Phylacteries. To counter the idolatrous practice of wearing amulets, Hebrew men began wearing *phylacteries.* There were two kinds of phylacteries: one worn on the forehead between the eyebrows, and one worn on the left arm. The one worn on the forehead was called a *frontlet.* It had four compartments, each of which contained a piece of parchment. On the first was written Exodus 13:1-10, on the second was written Exodus 13:11-16, on the third was written Deuteronomy 6:4-9, and on the fourth, Deuteronomy 11:13-21. These four pieces of paper were wrapped in animal skin, making a square pack. This small bundle was then tied to the forehead with a thong or ribbon. These Scripture passages contained God's commands to remember and obey His Law (e.g., Deut. 6:8).

The phylactery worn on a man's arm was made of two rolls of parchment, on which the laws were written in special ink. The parchment was partially rolled up, enclosed in a case of black calfskin, and tied with a thong to the upper left arm near the elbow. The thong was then wound crisscross around the arm, ending at the top of the middle finger. Some Jewish men wore their phylacteries both evening and morning; others wore them only at morning prayer. Phylacteries were not worn on the Sabbath or on other sacred days; those days were themselves holy signs, so the wearing of phylacteries was unnecessary.

Jesus condemned the practice of "making broad the phylacteries" (Matt. 23:5). The Pharisees made their phylacteries larger than usual, so that casual observers would think they were very holy.

D. Hair Style. Hebrew men considered the hair to be an important personal ornament, so they gave much care and attention to it. Egyptian and Assyrian monuments show examples of elaborate hair arrangements in those cultures. The Egyptians also wore various types of wigs. But we see an important difference between Hebrew and Egyptian hair styles in Genesis 41:14, which says that Joseph "shaved himself" before he was presented to the pharaoh. An Egyptian would have been content to comb his hair and trim his beard; but Hebrew men cut their hair much as modern Western men do, using a primitive kind of scissors (2 Sam. 14:26). The word *polled* in this text means "to cut the hair from the head." The Jews also used razors, as we see in Numbers 6:5.

When a Jewish man made a religious vow, he did not cut his

hair (cf. Judg. 13:5). The Israelites were not to shave their hair so closely that they resembled heathen gods who had shaved heads. Nor were they to resemble the Nazarites, who refused to cut their hair at all (Ezek. 44:20). In the New Testament times, long hair on men was considered to be contrary to nature (1 Cor. 11:14).

Men often applied perfumed oil to their hair before festivals or other joyous occasions (Psa. 23:5). Jesus mentions this custom in Luke 7:45, when He says, "My head with oil thou didst not anoint. . . ."

Jewish men also paid much attention to the care of the beard. It was an insult to attempt to touch a man's beard, except when kissing it respectfully and affectionately as a sign of friendship (2 Sam. 20:9). Tearing out the beard, cutting it off entirely, or neglecting to trim it were expressions of deep mourning (cf. Ezra 9:3; Isa. 15:2; Jer. 41:5). Egyptian and Roman men preferred clean-shaven faces, although Egyptian rulers did wear artificial beards.

E. Headdress. Apparently, Jewish men wore a headdress for special occasions (Isa. 61:3), on holidays, or in times of mourning (2 Sam. 15:30). We first see the headdress mentioned in Exodus 28:40, as a part of the priest's clothing.

Tunic. The tunic, a kimono-like inner garment reaching to the knees or ankles, was worn next to the skin. Both men and women wore tunics made from cotton, linen, or wool. Held close to the body by a *girdle* (usually a leather belt), the tunic might be the only garment worn by the poor in warm weather. However, the rich never appeared in public without their outer garments.

Hebrew men probably used a head covering only on rare occasions, though Egyptian and Assyrian men wore them often. Some ancient headdresses were quite elaborate, especially those worn by royalty. The common Egyptian man wore a simple headdress consisting of a square cloth, folded so that three corners hung down the back and shoulders. This may have been the type used by the Hebrews.

The Assyrians used a headdress much like a high turban (Ezek. 23:15). Syrian men in Damascus most likely wore the turban.

WOMEN'S CLOTHING

Women wore clothing that was very similar to that of men. However, the law strictly forbade a woman to wear anything that was thought to belong particularly to a man, such as the signet ring and other ornaments. According to the Jewish historian Josephus, women were also forbidden to use the weapons of a man. By the same token, men were forbidden to wear the outer robe of a woman (Deut. 22:5).

A. Inner Garment. This garment was worn by both sexes, and was made of wool, cotton, or linen.

B. Outer Garment. The Hebrew woman's outer garment differed from that of the man. It was longer, with enough border and fringe to cover the feet (Isa. 47:2; Jer. 13:22). It was secured at the waist by a girdle. As with the men, the female's clothing might be made of different materials, according to the social status of the individual.

The front of the woman's outer garment was long enough for her to tuck it up over the girdle to serve as an apron. The word *apron* is first mentioned in Genesis 3:7, when Adam and Eve sewed themselves aprons of fig leaves. This article of clothing may have resembled our modern apron to some degree. The apron might have been used to protect the clothing during work, or to carry some item (cf. Ruth 3:15).

C. Veil. Hebrew women did not wear a veil at all times, as is now the custom in many of the lands of the Near East.

Wearing a veil was an act of modesty that usually indicated that a woman was unmarried. When Rebekah first saw Isaac, she was not wearing a veil; but she covered herself with a veil before Isaac saw her (Gen. 24:65). Women of New Testament times covered their heads for worship, but not necessarily their faces (1 Cor. 11:5).

D. Handkerchief. The Hebrew word for *handkerchief (mispachoth)* might better be translated as *napkin* or *towel*. These cloths were used to wrap things being carried (Luke 19:20), to wipe perspiration from the face, or to cover the face of the dead.

Some commentators think that the burial napkin was tied under the chin and over the top of the head to keep the dead person's jaw from sagging (John 11:44). John 20:7 says that the napkin that covered the face of the Lord was found rolled and lying separately from the linen grave clothes.

Often the women of modern Near Eastern nations carry handkerchiefs with beautiful needlework. This may also have been the custom in ancient times.

E. Sandals. Jewish women wore sandals, as did the men. There were many variations of the common sandal. The sole might be made of the tough hide of a camel's neck. Sometimes several thicknesses of hide were sewn together.

One type of woman's sandal had two straps: one strap passed between the big toe and the second toe, and the other went around the heel and over the instep. This shoe could be easily slipped off when coming indoors.

F. Ornaments. The Bible first mentions women's jewelry when Abraham's servant presented earrings and bracelets to Rebekah (Gen. 24:22). Jeremiah well described the Jewish woman's attraction to jewelry when he said, "Can a maid forget her ornaments?" Hebrew women wore bracelets, necklaces, earrings, nose rings, and gold chains. Isaiah 3:16, 18:23 gives a graphic picture of the fashionably ornamented woman of Old Testament times.

1. Bracelets. Both Hebrew women and men wore bracelets (Gen. 24:30). Today, Near Eastern people consider a woman's bracelet to be a badge of high status or royalty, as it probably was in David's time (2 Sam. 1:10). The royal bracelet was probably made of a precious material, such as gold, and was worn above the elbow. The common woman's bracelet might have been worn at the wrist, as it is today (Ezek. 16:11).

Most women's bracelets were made in a full circle to slip over the hand. Some bracelets were made in two pieces that opened on a hinge and closed with a tie or pin. Bracelets varied in size, from several centimeters wide to slender bands.

2. Anklets. Women wore anklets as commonly as bracelets, and these were made of much the same materials (Isa. 3:16, 18, 20). Some anklets made a tinkling musical sound as the woman walked. Women of high rank wore hollow anklets filled with pebbles, so that the rattling sound could be heard when they walked.

3. Earrings. Among the Hebrews and Egyptians, only the women wore earrings (cf. Judg. 8:24). Among the Assyrians, both men and women wore earrings.

We are not certain of the form of Hebrew earrings, but Scripture passages suggest that they were round (e.g., Gen. 24:22). Egyptian earrings were generally large single hoops of gold, from 3 to 5 cm. (1 to 2 in.) in diameter. Occasionally, several hoops were fastened together or precious stones were added for effect.

Heathen nations sometimes used earrings as charms. (See the section on "Amulets.") We see this when Jacob's family went to Bethel from Shechem (Gen. 35:4), and they gave up their earrings.

4. Nose Jewels. The woman's nose ring or nose jewel was one of the most ancient ornaments of the East. The ring was made of ivory or precious metals, often with jewels in them. At times, these nose jewels were more than 6 cm. (2.5 in.) in diameter and hung down over the woman's lips. The custom of wearing nose rings still exists in some parts of the Near East, mainly among dancing girls and the lower class of people. However, we have no evidence that Hebrew women wore nose rings.

5. Crisping Pins. The Hebrew word *(charitim),* translated by the KJV as "crisping pins" in Isaiah 3:22 and as "bags" in 2

Kings 5:23, is used only these 2 times in the Bible. We are not sure what this type of jewelry might have been, or even whether it was a type of jewelry.

6. Cosmetics and Perfumes. Egyptian and Assyrian women used paint as a cosmetic. They colored their eyelashes and the edges of the eyelids with a fine black powder moistened with oil or vinegar, to achieve an effect somewhat like modern mascara.

Hebrew women also painted their eyelashes. But this practice was generally viewed with contempt, as was the case with Jezebel (2 Kings 9:30). Painting the eyes is disdainfully mentioned in Jeremiah 4:30 and Ezekiel 23:40.

Some women stained their fingers and toes with henna. This was especially true of the Egyptian women, who also tattooed their hands, feet, and face.

Ancient women used perfume in much the same manner as women do today. Common sources of perfume in Bible times were frankincense and myrrh from Arabia and Africa, aloes and nard from India, cinnamon from Aylon, galbanum from Persia, and stacte and saffron from Palestine. Perfume was a valued item of trade (cf. Gen. 37:25).

Exodus 30:4-38 tells how the Hebrews made a perfume used in the tabernacle rituals. But the Law forbade the personal use of this perfume.

7. Hair Style. Paul the apostle said that hair was a natural veil, or covering, for the woman; he indicates that in his day it was shameful for a Christian woman to cut her hair (1 Cor. 11:15). The women wore their hair long and braided. The Talmud mentions that Jewish women used combs and hairpins.

Among the Egyptian and Assyrian women, the hair styles were much more elaborate than those worn by the Hebrews, as the monuments of that day show.

8. Headdress. Jewish women used the headdress to some degree, but the apostle Paul urged modest apparel for Christian women (1 Tim. 2:8). The women may have used gold or jewels for hair ornaments (1 Pet. 3:3), as was the practice of women in neighboring countries.

The veil that Jewish women sometimes wore could hardly be considered a headdress, although it did cover the head. In contrast, the headdress for other Near Eastern women was elaborate and costly, depending on the wealth and social position of the wearer.

PRIESTS' CLOTHING

Priestly dress was much different from that of the common Jew. Furthermore, the high priest's clothing differed from that of the common priest.

A. Breeches. Among the Hebrews, breeches were worn only by the priests. In some neighboring countries, both breeches and trousers were worn by common men.

The Jews used fine linen to make this priestly garment. Apparently, it served as an undergarment so that the priest would not be exposed when he climbed the steps of the temple to minister at the altar (Exod. 28:42-43). This undergarment covered the priest's body from the waist to the knees. Rather than being trousers, "breeches" were probably a double apron. Other references to "breeches" are found in Exodus 39:28; Leviticus 6:10; 16:4; and Ezekiel 44:18.

B. Cassock or Robe. The priests also wore robes of white linen during their temple ministrations. These garments came from the weaver seamless, bound at the waist with a girdle decorated by needlework (Exod. 28:31-34). The garment of Jesus was also a seamless robe, symbolically showing His universal priesthood (John 19:23; Heb. 4:14-15). The priest's robe nearly covered the feet and was woven in a diamond or chessboard pattern.

C. Bonnet. A bonnet was worn by the ordinary priest. This bonnet was made of fine linen (Exod. 39:28). The Hebrew word *(migbaoth)* from which *bonnet* was translated means "to be lofty."

D. Footwear. During all of their ministrations, the priests were to be barefoot. Before they entered the tabernacle, they were to wash their hands and feet. "And he set the laver between the tent of the congregation and the altar, and put water there, to wash withal. And Moses and Aaron and his sons washed their hands and their feet thereat" (Exod. 40:30-31). The area on which the priests were standing was considered holy ground, as was the case with Moses and the burning bush (Exod. 3:5).

E. Hair Care. In Leviticus 21:5, we see that baldness disqualified a man from the priesthood. The priest was not allowed to shave his head or rip his clothes, even to mourn his mother or father's death (Lev. 21:10-11).

HIGH PRIEST'S CLOTHING

One of the distinctions that separated the high priest from the common priest was the sprinkling of his garments with anointing oil (Exod. 28:41; 29:21). The high priest's clothes were passed on to his successor at his death.

Making clothes. Clothing worn by the Hebrews served as the external symbol of the individual's innermost feelings and desires. Festive and joyful occasions called for bright colors, while the Jew in mourning put on sackcloth, the poorest kind of dress. Israelite families made most of their own clothing. In this family scene, the father is making leather sandals while the mother sews a robe from material she has woven.

The high priest's garments consisted of 7 parts—the ephod, the robe of the ephod, the breastplate, the mitre, the embroidered coat, the girdle, and the breeches (Exod. 28:42).

A. Ephod. The high priest's garments were made of plain linen (1 Sam. 2:18; 2 Sam. 6:14), as were the clothes for all priests. But his ephod was made of "gold, of blue, and of purple, of scarlet, and of fine twined linen" (Exod. 28:6). This indicates that it was a blend of wool and linen, since linen could be dyed only blue. The "cunning work" signifies some type of embroidery.

There were two parts to the ephod: one covering the back and the other covering the breast of the wearer. The garment was fastened at each shoulder by a large onyx stone.

The girdle of the ephod was made of blue, purple, and scarlet fabric interwoven with gold thread (Exod. 28:8).

B. Robe of the Ephod. The robe of the ephod was of inferior material to the ephod, dyed blue (Exod. 39:22). It was worn under the ephod and was longer than the ephod. This robe had no sleeves, only slits in the sides for the arms.

The skirt of this garment had a fringe (trimming) of pomegranates in blue, purple, and scarlet, with a bell of gold hung between each pomegranate. These bells were attached to the bottom of the high priest's robe so that he would be heard as he came or went from the holy place (Exod. 28:32-35).

C. Breastplate. The high priest's breastplate is described in detail in Exodus 28:15-30. It was a piece of embroidered material about 25.4 cm. (10 in.) square and doubled over to make a bag or pouch.

This priestly garment was adorned with twelve precious stones, each bearing the name of one of the twelve tribes of Israel (Exod. 28:9-12). The two upper corners were fastened to the ephod, from which it was not to be loosened (Exod. 28:28). The two lower corners were fastened to the girdle. The rings, chains, and other fastenings were of gold or rich lace.

The breastplate and ephod were called a "memorial" (Exod. 28:12,29), because they reminded the priest of his relationship to the twelve tribes of Israel. It was also called the "breastplate of judgment" (Exod. 28:15), possibly because it was worn by the priest, who was God's spokesman of justice and judgment to the Jewish nation. It may also have been called this because it provided a container for the *urim* and *thummim*, the sacred lots, that showed God's judgments upon men (cf. Num. 26:55; Josh. 7:14; 14:2; 1 Sam. 14:42).

D. Mitre. The mitre, or upper turban, was the official headdress of the high priest (Exod. 28:39). It was made of fine linen, had many folds, and had a total length of about 7.3 m. (8 yds.).

This long cloth was wound around the head in turban style. On the front of the mitre was a gold plate bearing the Hebrew words for "Holiness unto the Lord" (Exod. 28:43-48; 39:28, 30).

E. Embroidered Coat, Girdle, and Breeches. This particular coat was long-skirted, made of linen, and embroidered with a pattern as if stones were set in it (Exod. 28:4). The common priests also wore this garment.

The girdle of the high priest's garments was wound around the body several times from the breast downwards. The ends of the girdle hung down to the ankles (Exod. 29:5). Beneath the priestly garments, the high priest wore the same type of breeches as did the common priest.

Coat. The coat was an outer robe with sleeves. The girdle—sometimes ornamented with precious metals, stones, or embroidery—held this garment close to the body.

9

ARCHITECTURE AND FURNITURE

Modern people admire the architecture of classical Greece and Rome, with its soaring marble pillars and elaborately decorated arches. But Israel produced very little architecture that we would call innovative or awe-inspiring. The Israelites designed their buildings and furniture to serve their daily needs, giving little thought to esthetic features. Yet their buildings and furniture tell us something of the people's way of life.

The most common dwellings in the ancient world were tents, formed by setting poles in the ground and stretching a covering of cloth or skin over them. The tent dweller would use cords to fasten this covering to stakes driven in the ground (cf. Isa. 54:2). Sometimes people used curtains to divide their tents into rooms and covered the ground with mats or carpets. The door was a fold of cloth that could be dropped or raised. The tent dweller kindled his fire in a hole in the middle of the tent floor. His cooking utensils were very few and simple, and were easily moved from place to place.

When people began settling in cities, they built more permanent homes. Apparently they developed skills of architecture at a very early period. But even while the Canaanites and Assyrians built cities, the Hebrews lived in tents; it was not until the conquest of the Promised Land that they abandoned their simple habits. Then they entered the houses that the Canaanites left.

The Bible tells us that the Israelites built large and costly houses in Judea (cf. Jer. 22:14; Amos 3:15; Hag. 1:4). But these houses belonged to wealthy people; many still lived in tents or very crude shelters.

Wealthy people built their houses in the form of a cloister, that is, surrounding an open court. A person entered the house by a door which was ordinarily kept locked, and was tended by someone who acted as a porter (cf. Acts 12:13). This door opened into a porch, furnished with seats or benches. One then walked through the porch to a short flight of stairs leading to the chambers and the open quadrangular court.

THE CENTRAL COURT

The court was the center of a Jewish house. Probably this is where Jesus sat when a group of men lowered a paralytic man "into the midst" to reach Him (Luke 5:19). The court was designed to admit light and air to the rooms around it. Tile or rock paved the floor of the court to shed rain that might come in through the skylight. Sometimes the homeowner built this court around a fountain or well (cf. 2 Sam. 17:18).

Crowds gathered in a host's court on festive occasions (cf. Esther 1:5). Usually the host would provide carpets, mats, and chairs for his guests, and might even stretch an awning over the skylight.

The surrounding rooms opened only onto the court, so that a person had to cross the court when entering or leaving the house. In later centuries, builders began erecting balconies or galleries outside the rooms that faced the central court.

A simple stairway of stone or wood led from the court to the rooms above, and to the roof. Larger houses might have more than one set of stairs.

A. The Master's Quarters. On the side of the court that faced the entrance was the reception room of the master of the house. It was furnished handsomely with a raised platform and a couch on three sides, which was a bed by night and a seat by day. The guests who entered took off their sandals before stepping upon the raised portion of the room.

The rooms assigned to the wife and daughters were usually upstairs, but sometimes they were on the level of the central court. No one except the master of the house could enter these apartments. Because the owner bestowed the greatest expense upon these rooms, they were sometimes called "palaces of the house" (1 Kings 16:18; 2 Kings 15:25) or "the house of the women" (Esther 2:3; cf. 1 Kings 7:8-12).

B. Domestic Quarters. We suppose that in ancient Judea, as in Palestine today, the people used their ground floor for domestic purposes—storing food, housing the servants, and so on. These ground-floor rooms were small and crudely furnished.

THE UPPER ROOMS

When a person ascended to the second story by the stairs, he found that the chambers were large and airy, and often furnished with much more elegance than the rooms below. These upper rooms were also higher and larger than the lower rooms, projecting over the lower part of the building so that their windows hung over the street. They were secluded, spacious, and very comfortable.

Sketch of a house. This drawing depicts a large residence in an ancient Israelite village. The house of the average Israelite was small and uncomfortable by modern standards. A favorite spot for relaxation was the roof, reached by a stone staircase or a simple wooden ladder.

Paul preached his farewell sermon in such a room. We can imagine that the crowd had to stand in two circles or ranks, the outer circle being next to the wall and lying on cushions beside the window casement. In that position Eutychus went to sleep and fell into the street (Acts 20:7-12).

A. The Alliyah. The Jews sometimes built another structure called the *alliyah* over the porch or gateway of the house. It consisted of only one or two rooms, and rose one story above the main house. The householder used it to entertain strangers, to store wardrobes, or for rest and meditation. Jesus probably referred to the *alliyah* when He spoke of going into the "closet" to pray (Matt. 6:6). Steps led directly from the street to the *alliyah*, but another flight of stairs connected the *alliyah* with the central court of the house. The *alliyah* afforded a much more private place for worship than the main roof of the house, which might be occupied by the whole family.

The Bible may refer to the *alliyah* when it mentions the "little chamber" of Elisha (2 Kings 4:10), the "summer chamber" of Eglon (Judg. 3:20-23), the "chamber over the gate" (2 Sam. 18:33), the "upper chamber" of Ahaz (2 Kings 23:12), and the "inner chamber" where Ben-hadad hid himself (1 Kings 20:30).

B. The Roof. The roof was an important part of a house in biblical times. A person could climb to the roof by a flight of stairs along the outside wall. In most cases the roof was flat; but sometimes the builders made domes over the more important rooms. Jewish law required each house to have a balustrade or railing around the roof to keep anyone from falling off (Deut. 22:8). Adjoining houses often shared the same roof, and low walls on the roof marked the borders of each house.

The builders covered roofs with a type of cement that hardened under the sun. If this cracked, the householder had to spread a layer of grass on the roof to keep out the rain (cf. 2 Kings 19:26; Psa. 129:6). Some houses had tiles or flat bricks on the roof.

The Israelites used their roofs as a place of retreat and meditation (Neh. 8:16; 2 Sam. 11:2; Isa. 15:3; 22:1; Jer.

Window balustrade. Found at Ramat Rahel in southern Israel, this row of limestone pillars (*ca.* 600 B.C.) appears to have been a window balustrade. It was probably painted red, since traces of red paint were found on the pieces from which these columns were reconstructed. The pillars once graced King Jehoiakim's palace.

48:38). They dried linen, flax, corn, figs and other fruits on the rooftops (Josh. 2:6). Sometimes they pitched tents on their roofs and slept there at night (2 Sam. 16:22).

The people used their rooftops for private conferences (1 Sam. 9:25). They also went there for private worship (Jer. 19:3; 2 Kings 23:12; Zeph. 1:5; Acts 10:9) and to shout public announcements or bewail the loss of loved ones (Jer. 48:38; Luke 12:3).

WINDOWS AND DOORS

In ancient houses, the windows were simply rectangular holes in the wall that opened upon the central court or upon the street outside. Sometimes the Israelites built a projecting balcony or porch along the front of the house, carefully enclosed by latticework. They opened the balcony window only for festivals and other special occasions. We suppose that Jezebel was looking out such an outer window when she was seized and put to death by Jehu (2 Kings 9:30-33). This window was probably called the "casement" (Prov. 7:6; Song of Sol. 2:9). The Israelites had no glass windows because glass was so expensive.

The doors of ancient houses were not hung on hinges. The jam (or inner side-piece) of the door projected as a circular shaft at the top and bottom. The upper end of this shaft would fit into a socket in the lintel and the lower end fell into a socket in the threshold. The King James Version loosely uses the word *hinges* in referring to the shaft of the door (1 Kings 7:50; Prov. 26:14).

Often builders equipped the main door of the house with a lock and key. These ancient keys were made of wood or metal, and some were so large that they were conspicuous when carried in public (Isa. 22:22). Treasurers or other civic officers carried these huge keys as a symbol of their high office.

FIREPLACES

Ancient houses had no chimneys, even though some versions of the Bible use this word in Hosea 13:3. Smoke from the hearth escaped through holes in the roof and walls. The hearth itself was not a permanent fixture; it was a small metal stove or brazier (cf. Jer. 36:22-23). Since the hearth was easy to carry from place to place, kings and generals often used it on military campaigns.

Table from Jericho. A tomb in Jericho contained this long table with two legs at one end and one at the other.

The Parthenon

The Parthenon in Athens is one of the finest examples of classic Greek architecture. It physically represents the ancient Greeks' rational, harmonious approach to life. Moreover, it is a marvel of architectural design.

The Greeks erected at least one previous structure on the site of the Parthenon in 488 B.C., when they laid out a massive structure as a thank-offering for their victory over the Persians at Marathon. The limestone foundation for this building extended over 6 m. (20 ft.) into the rock of the Acropolis. Most above-ground work on this site was destroyed, however, when the Persians sacked the Acropolis in 480 B.C.

The Greeks began work on the Parthenon in 447 B.C. and completed it in 438 B.C. They made the structure the main temple on the Acropolis around 432 B.C., when they dedicated it to Athena Parthenos, patron goddess of Athens. Construction on this building was funded by the government of Pericles.

The building was designed to create an optical illusion. The tops of the Parthenon's Doric columns lean toward the center of each colonnade, the steps curve upward at the center, and the columns are more widely spaced at the center of each row than at the end. This makes the columns appear to be evenly spaced. (If they had truly been evenly spaced, the perspective angle would have made them look uneven.)

There are 8 columns at each end of the Parthenon and 17 on each side. The Parthenon has a central area, or *cella,* which in turn is divided into chambers. An inner colonnade originally held the great cult statue of Athena, a masterpiece of the sculptor Phidias. This statue has not survived, but we know of its general appearance through smaller copies and through many representations on ancient coins. This statue was seen and described by Greek traveler Pausanias in the second century A.D.

The entire Parthenon is made of marble, including the tiles on the roof. The Greeks used no mortar or cement on the structure; they fitted marble blocks together with the greatest accuracy and secured them with metal clamps and dowels.

An ornamental band of low relief sculpture *(frieze)* decorates the Parthenon. These decorations represent combat among the gods such as Zeus, Athena, and Poseidon. They also picture mounted horsemen, chariot groups, and citizens of Athens.

The Greeks used color to highlight the Parthenon's beauty. The ceiling of the colonnade was colored with red, blue, and gold or yellow. A band running next to the frieze was colored red, and color accented the sculpture and bronze accessories within the Parthenon.

The Parthenon had a varied history. As early as 298 B.C., Lachares stripped the gold plates from the statue of Athena. In A.D. 426 the Parthenon was converted into a Christian church, and the Turks turned it into a mosque in 1460. In 1687 the Venetians, who were battling the Greeks, used the Parthenon as a powder magazine, and accidentally set off an explosion that destroyed the central section of the building. No major repairs were made until 1950, when engineers put fallen columns back in place and repaired the northern colonnade.

METHODS OF CONSTRUCTION

We have been describing a typical house of the wealthy people. Individual houses varied from this floor plan; some were more elaborate than this, and others were simpler. But the Israelites used traditional methods of construction in all their homes.

Stables. Archaeologists discovered these ruins of an extensive complex of stables, capable of housing as many as 480 horses at Megiddo. This is the northern stable compound consisting of five units, each accommodating about twenty-four horses. Excavators first attributed these stables to Solomon: but subsequent investigation has shown that they date from the time of Ahab, several generations later.

A. Homes of the Wealthy. The materials for building were abundant in Palestine. Well-to-do homeowners could easily obtain stone and brick and the best timber for ornamental work in their houses. They often used hewn stone (Amos 5:11) and highly polished marble (1 Chron. 29:2; Esther 1:6). They also used large quantities of cedar for their wall paneling and ceilings, often with moldings of gold, silver, and ivory (Jer. 22:14; Hag. 1:4). Perhaps their fondness for ivory accounts for the Bible's references to "houses of ivory" and "ivory palaces" (e.g., 1 Kings 22:39; Psa. 35:8; Amos 3:15).

Wealthy landowners also built "winter houses" and "summer houses" for their comfort in those seasons (cf. Amos 3:15). They built the summer houses partly underground and paved them with marble. These houses generally had fountains in the central court, and were constructed to bring in currents of fresh air. This made them very refreshing in the torrid heats of summer. We know little about the construction of the winter houses.

We get a glimpse of a typical construction method of Old Testament times when we read how Samson destroyed a temple of the Philistines (Judg. 16:23-30). Samson's enemies brought him into the central court of the temple, which was surrounded by a range of balconies, each supported by one or two pillars. Here the officers of state assembled to transact public business and give public entertainments. If the pillars collapsed, it would upset the building and the people standing on the balconies would tumble to the pavement below.

B. Homes of the Poor. The houses of the common people were hovels of only one room with mud walls. The builders reinforced these walls with reeds and rushes, or with stakes plastered with clay. So the walls were very insecure, and often became breeding places for serpents and vermin (cf. Amos 5:19). The family occupied the same room with their animals, although they sometimes slept on a platform above the animals. Their windows were small holes high in the wall, perhaps barred.

The Bible warns against "leprosy in the house" (Lev. 14:34-53), which was probably a chemical reaction in the mud walls of these poorer homes. The Israelites understood that this "leprosy" would harm their health, so the priests ordered them to remove it.

The peasants made the doors of their homes very low and a person had to stoop to enter them. This kept out wild beasts and enemies. Some say it was a means of preventing the roving bands of Arabs from riding into the houses.

THE SERVICE OF DEDICATION

The Israelites dedicated their new homes before they set up housekeeping in them (Deut. 20:5). We suppose they celebrated this event with great joy, and asked God's blessing upon the house and the people who would live in it.

FURNITURE

To our eyes, the best-furnished houses of Palestine would have appeared empty. On the marble floors of a rich man's house we would have seen beautiful rugs, and on the benches cushions of rich fabric. But the wealthy Israelites did not have the great variety of furniture to which we are accustomed, and

The Herodium

The Herodium. Herod the Great built magnificent structures for his own comfort and protection. Among these projects were his palace-fortress at Masada and the Herodium. In the event of insurrection or military defeat, either would offer strong defense. The Herodium, which was also designed to be Herod's burial place, stands as a tribute to Herod's obsessive fear. It is one of the largest fortresses ever built to guard one man.

The Herodium stands about 11 km. (7 mi.) south of Jerusalem and 5 km. (3 mi.) southeast of Bethlehem, at an altitude of about 700 m. (2300 ft.). It was built on the spot where Herod defeated the forces of the Hasmoneans and their supporters in 40 B.C.—a place of fond memories for Herod. The first-century Jewish historian Josephus tells of the construction of the Herodium in 20 B.C., and of Herod's funeral procession to the site. It was one of the last three strongholds remaining in Jewish hands outside Jerusalem when the Romans destroyed that city in A.D. 70. The Herodium also served as a rebel center during the Bar-Cochba revolt (A.D. 132–135).

V. Corbo led four seasons of excavation at the Herodium (1962–1967). G. Foerster did restoration and exploration at the site of the Herodium 1967 and 1970, and E. Netzer led a dig at the site in 1972. Together they uncovered an astonishing structure that was surely the greatest engineering feat of intertestamental times.

Viewed from afar, the site looks like a shortened cone. The structure consists of four towers—three semicircular and one round—surrounded by a circular curtain wall, the outer diameter of which is 55 m. (180 ft.). This double wall has a 3-m. (10-ft.) wide passageway between walls. Evidently sand and stone building debris were piled around the outside of the walls soon after construction, leaving only their tops exposed. Thus the hill took on a conical shape.

The eastern half of the Herodium's inner space consisted of an open courtyard surrounded by Corinthian columns, with an *exedra* (outdoor area with seats for informal conversations) on each end. The western half included an elaborately decorated bathhouse complex, with a group of rooms including a dining room occupying the southern side. The dining room was converted into a synagogue, evidently when some of Bar-Kochba's followers held out there in the second century. Above the western rooms rose a second and possibly even a third story, used as living quarters.

A network of huge cisterns honeycombed the interior of the hill. An aqueduct brought water to the site from Solomon's Pools near Bethlehem. One of the inscribed pieces of pottery found by archaeologists at the site mentions Herod.

At the northern base of the hill Netzer uncovered a complex of structures. There was a palace measuring about 53 m. x 122 m. (175 ft. x 400 ft.), from which extended an observation balcony over what appears to have been a hippodrome about 300 m. (1,000 ft.) long, a pool, service building, and other unidentified structures. Obviously, Herod intended to live in style and be buried in splendor.

the poor people had even less. A well-to-do man might have a mat or a skin to recline on during the day, a mattress to sleep on at night, a stool, a low table, and a brazier—this would be the extent of his furniture. Notice that the rich Shunammite woman furnished the room of Elisha with only a bed (perhaps merely a mattress), a table, a stool, and a candlestick (2 Kings 4:10-13).

Because the floors of a more fashionable home were of tile or plaster, they often needed sweeping or scrubbing (cf. Matt. 22:11; Luke 15:8). At night the residents threw down thick, coarse mattresses to sleep on. The poorer people used skins for the same purpose. On 2 or 3 sides of the rich man's room was a bench, generally 30 cm. (12 in.) high, covered with a stuffed cushion. The master sat upon this bench in the daytime; but at one end of the room it was more elevated, and this was the usual place for sleeping (cf. 2 Kings 1:4; 4:10). Besides the bench, the very wealthy people had bedsteads made of wood, ivory, or other expensive materials (Amos 6:4; Deut. 3:11). These bedsteads became more common in New Testament times (cf. Mark 4:21).

The Israelites used some of their normal outer garments for bedclothes (Exod. 22:26-27; Deut. 24:12-13). Before lying down for the night, they would simply take off their sandals and their girdle. The pillow of the Hebrews was probably a goat skin stuffed with wool, feathers, or some other soft material. The poorer people of Palestine use these skins for their pillows today.

Kings and other rulers required a stool for their feet when they sat upon a throne (2 Chron. 9:18), but this piece of furniture was rare in private homes.

On the other hand, lamps were very common. They burned olive oil, pitch, naphtha, or wax, and they had wicks of cotton or flax. (A Jewish tradition says that the priests made wicks for the lamps of the temple from their old linen garments.) The poorer Israelites made their lamps of clay, while the wealthy had lamps of bronze and other metals.

The Israelites let their lamps burn all night, since light made them feel safer. We are told that the family would rather go without food than let their lamps go out, since that indicated they had deserted their house. So when Job predicts the ruin of wicked people, he says, ". . . The light of the wicked is put out . . . The lamp is dark in his tent, and his lamp above him is put out" (Job 18:5-6, RSV). The writer of Proverbs praises the prudent wife by saying, "Her lamp does not go out at night" (Prov. 31:18). Several other Bible passages show that the lamp symbolized the life and dignity of a family (cf. Job 21:17; Jer. 25:10).

Though their furniture was simple, the Israelites lived in much more comfort than their ancestors, who wandered with their flocks. In Jesus' day the typical home was neat and clean, with the functional beauty common to homes in other countries influenced by the Hellenistic culture. Though Palestine was ruled by Rome, few people adopted the ornate tastes of the Romans.

Bronze fittings for bed. This bed from Tell el-Far'ah in southern Israel has been reconstructed from bronze fittings for the legs and the iron tie-rods that held the legs together. Most Israelites slept on pallets or mats upon the floor. Only the wealthy could afford the luxury of beds, which became more common in New Testament times.

10

MUSIC

The Bible gives very little information about Hebrew musical forms and how they developed. For this reason, we must combine Bible study with history and archaeology if we wish to learn about the music of Bible times.

THE DEVELOPMENT OF HEBREW MUSIC

The history of Hebrew music goes back to the first person who beat a stick on a rock, and it extends to the temple orchestra and the "joyous sound" called for in Psalm 150. That first musician heard rhythm as he beat his primitive instrument. As people began to realize they could make music, they created more complex instruments.

For example, David is credited with inventing a number of instruments, although we do not know precisely what they were (cf. Amos 6:5). David called upon a chorus of 4,000 to offer praises to the Lord "with the instruments which I made . . . to praise" (1 Chron. 23:5; cf. 2 Chron. 7:6; Neh. 12:6). David also composed songs, such as his lament over the death of Saul and Jonathan.

Though God directed Israel's social and religious development, the nation absorbed ideas from surrounding cultures. Israel was at a geographical crossroads and was exposed to ideas and customs from other parts of the world (Gen. 37:25), including musical style.

Many men of Israel married foreign wives whose customs gradually crept into Hebrew lifestyle. According to the collection of post-biblical Jewish writings called the *Midrash*, King Solomon married an Egyptian woman whose dowry included

1,000 musical instruments. If this is true, no doubt she brought musicians with her to play those instruments in the traditional Egyptian way.

The purpose the music served and the way in which listeners responded to it also influenced the development of Hebrew music. In times of war, it was often necessary to sound an alarm or send some other kind of urgent signal. Thus the Hebrews developed the *shophar,* an instrument like a trumpet with loud, piercing tones (Exod. 32:17-18; Judg. 7:18-20). Merrymaking and frivolity called for the light, happy tones produced by the pipe or flute (Gen. 31:27; Judges 11:34-35; Matt. 9:23-24; Luke 15:23-25).

A. Distracting Effect. Hebrew leaders who ministered in the temple took great care to avoid using music that was associated with sensuous pagan worship. In cultures where fertility rites were common, women singers and musicians incited sexual orgies in honor of their gods. Even instruments not associated with pagan practices were sometimes restricted. For example, priests feared that a happy, melodious flute tune in the temple could distract someone's mind from worship. The prophet Amos condemned those "who sing idle songs to the sound of the harp" (Amos 6:5, RSV).

Of course, there were times when the distractions of music could be helpful. The soothing strains of David's lyre refreshed a tormented Saul (1 Sam. 16:23). After Daniel was shut up in the den of lions, King Darius retired to his room and refused to let the "instruments of music" be brought to him (Dan. 6:18).

Music was an important part of everyday life. Merrymaking, weddings, and funerals were not complete without music. Even war relied on music, since special instruments sounded the call to battle. Aristocratic diversion and relaxation patronized the musicians and their skills.

B. Function in Worship. Music was also a part of the religious life of Israel. The Israelites' formal worship observed various rituals prescribed by God. Music served as an accompaniment to these rituals.

Temple music consisted of singers and an orchestra. The

singers and musicians could come only from the males of certain families. Likewise, the types of instruments were restricted. Instruments that were associated with women, with raucous merrymaking (such as the Egyptian *sistrum*), or with pagan worship were banned from the temple orchestra.

The Old Testament lists several kinds of instruments in the temple orchestra (cf. 1 Chron. 15:28; 16:42; 25:1). These instruments include the big harp *(nevel)*, the lyre *(kinnor)*, the ram's horn *(shophar)*, the trumpet *(chatsotserah)*, the timbrel *(toph)*, and cymbals *(metsiltayim)*. After the Israelites returned from the Exile and rebuilt the temple, the orchestra was reestablished (cf. Neh. 12:27). The pipe or flute *(halil)* was probably now included, and vocal music became more prominent.

Beyond formal worship within the temple, music was a part of other religious activities. Instruments not allowed in the temple were played at other religious functions, such as feast days. Often the feast began with a musical proclamation; then music, singing, and even dancing were part of the celebration. Women singers and musicians were allowed to participate (Ezra 2:65; Neh. 7:76; 2 Chron. 35:25).

C. Limits of Our Knowledge. The Old Testament seldom mentions the forms of music, the origins of instruments, and so on. The way to play or make instruments was passed on by oral tradition rather than written record. Most of that oral tradition has been lost, leaving us with only the brief information in the Bible.

Horn and drum players. This basalt relief from Carchemish in Syria (eighth or ninth century B.C.) depicts four musicians, one blowing a curved horn, one carrying a large drum, and two beating the drum with their open hands. The figure at right appears to wear a neckstrap to help support the drum.

Very few ancient musical instruments exist intact, so we must guess at how they looked and sounded. By comparing Scripture references with the artifacts of other cultures, historians and archaeologists have helped fill in many of the gaps in our knowledge of music in Bible times.

This study is a continuing process, as newer translations of the Bible demonstrate. If we compare passages about music from the King James Version with more recent translations, some differences can be noted. The following lists of instruments give the name in the KJV for each instrument mentioned, along with the findings of more recent interpretation.

TYPES OF INSTRUMENTS

Musical instruments fall into three basic classes, according to the way the sound is produced: (1) stringed instruments, which use vibrating strings to produce the sound; (2) percussion instruments, in which the sound is produced by a vibrating membrane or metal shell; and (3) wind instruments, which produce sound by passing air over a vibrating reed.

A. Percussion Instruments. The people of Israel used a variety of percussion instruments to sound out the rhythm of their music. Rhythm was the vital element of their poetry and songs.

1. Bells. One kind of bell had a name *(metsilloth)* that came from the Hebrew word meaning "to jingle" or "to rattle." This type of bell is mentioned only once in the Bible (Zech. 14:20), where we are told that the Israelites attached these bells to the bridle or breast strap of horses.

Another kind of bell was a tiny, pure gold bell *(paamonim)*. It was fastened to the hem of the high priest's robe and alternated with ornamental pomegranates (Exod. 28:33-34). These bells produced a sound only when they touched one another, for they did not have clappers. This jingling sound signified that the high priest was coming before God; others who dared to enter the holy of holies would be slain (v. 35).

2. Castanets. *See* "Cymbals" and "Rattler-Sistrum."

Egyptian musicians. This tomb painting from Thebes (*ca.* fifteenth century B.C.) portrays Egyptian women playing musical instruments and dancing. From left to right we see a harpist, a lutist, a young dancer, a player of the double pipe, and a lyrist with a seven-stringed instrument. Notice the leopard skin decorating the lower part of the harp frame.

3. Cymbals. Cymbals (*metziltayim* or *tziltzal*) were made of copper and were the only percussion instruments in the temple orchestra. They were used when the people were celebrating and praising God. They joined with trumpets and singers to express joy and thanks to the Lord (1 Chron. 15:16; 16:5). Asaph, David's chief musician (1 Chron. 16:5), was a cymbal player. When the people returned from captivity, Asaph's descendants were called to join singers and trumpets in praise to the Lord (Ezra 3:10).

In passages such as 1 Chronicles 16:5, some versions translate the Hebrew as *castanets*. It is now generally believed that this is inaccurate and should be *cymbals*.

4. Rattler-Sistrum. This is the correct translation for 2 Samuel 6:5. (The RSV uses *castanets*, while the KJV uses *coronet*.) The sistrum was a small U-shaped frame with a handle attached at the bottom of the curve. Pieces of metal or other small objects were strung on small bars stretched from one side of the sistrum to the other.

The use of the sistrum goes back to ancient Egypt and has counterparts in other ancient cultures. It was merely a noise-maker, played by women on both joyous and sad occasions.

5. Tabret. *See* "Timbrel."

6. Timbrel. Modern musicians would classify this instrument as a "membranophone" because the sound is produced by a vibrating membrane. It is correctly translated as either *timbrel* or *tambourine.* (KJV uses the term *tabret.*) It was carried and beaten by the hand. In very early times it may have been made with two membranes, with pieces of bronze inserted in the rim.

7. Gong. The "brass" mentioned in 1 Corinthians 13:1 was actually a metal gong. It was used for weddings and other joyous occasions.

B. Stringed Instruments. Archaeologists have found fragments of harps and other stringed instruments from Egypt and neighboring countries of the Near East. Scripture describes several stringed instruments that were used in Israel.

1. Dulcimer. This term appears in the Bible only in Daniel 3:5, 7, 10, and 15. It is not a precise translation. *See* "Harp."

2. Harp. The harp (KJV also uses *psaltery, viol,* or *dulcimer*) was a favorite instrument of the aristocratic class and was lavishly made (1 Kings 10:12; 2 Chron. 9:11). It was used in the temple orchestra and was appointed to "raise sounds of joy" (1 Chron. 15:16).

Lute. This terra cotta plaque from Iraq (*ca.* 2000 B.C.) depicts a musician playing a three-stringed triangular lute. The lute was usually played by women and may have been one of the "instruments of music" mentioned in 1 Samuel 18:6.

The World's Oldest Sheet Music?

One scholar recently uncovered controversial evidence suggesting that the ancient Egyptians produced written sheet music during the same centuries as the building of the mighty Sphinx, about 4500 years ago. Maureen M. Barwise claims to have deciphered musical hieroglyphs that date back as far as the fourth dynasty of the old kingdom, roughly 2600 B.C.[1]

According to her translation, the music was written basically in a single melodic line. The earliest sacred pieces featured harps and flutes accompanied by timbrels and percussion sticks, joined later by trumpets, lutes, and lyres.

Ms. Barwise claims the Egyptian musicians used a "gapped" scale, producing music that was beautiful in spite of obvious peculiarities. She notes that it was similar to ancient Gaelic, Welsh, and Scottish folk tunes, with melodies like the droning of the Highland bagpipe.

The researcher undertook the unusual task of reproducing a number of tunes, translating them into the treble-clef keyboard. According to Barwise, the Egyptians understood timing, pitch, rhythm, and harmonic chords in addition to basic melody. The adapted tunes seem to cover a variety of musical moods, from the somewhat playful "Beautiful Moon-Bird of the Nile" to the rather stately grand march, "Honor to the Strong Arm of Pharaoh."

Egyptian music was considered sacred. Therefore, its composition was strictly governed by law and did not develop greatly over the centuries.

Wall paintings, bas reliefs, and the literature of antiquity clearly show that the Egyptians were skillful musicians. Many experts believe that this early music was preserved in written form, but established archaeological theory holds that the melodies were an oral tradition.

Ms. Barwise's translation of hieroglyphics into music notation challenges the old school of thought and her scholarship has met mixed acceptance. Some critics agree with David Wulston's evaluation, that her work is nothing more than "a whimsical Tolikein-like fantasy [constructed] out of the most unpromising material."[2]

3. Lute. This 3-stringed triangular instrument may have been one of the "instruments of music" mentioned in 1 Samuel 18:6. It was usually played by women and was excluded from the temple orchestra.

4. Lyre. Two Hebrew terms are translated as *lyre*. (The KJV uses *harp*.) One is mentioned in only one book of the Bible (Dan. 3:5, 7, 10, 15). This particular lyre *(nevel)* was frequently used for secular music, such as the merrymaking at Nebuchadnezzar's banquet. It was played by plucking the strings with the fingers.

A smaller lyre *(kinnor)* was considered to be the most sophisticated instrument. Its shape and number of strings varied, but all types of lyres produced a most pleasing sound. The lyre was used in secular settings (Isa. 23:16), but was welcomed in sacred use too. It was the instrument David used to soothe King Saul. Generally, this "little lyre" was played by

Story Music

On the surface, the music of the ancient Greeks and Hebrews seemed to have little in common. The Greeks sang of their gods and mythological battles; the Hebrews, on the other hand, devoted their songs to praising the one God. But there is an important link between Greek and Hebrew music, one that involves poetry, song, and religion. That link is the *epic.*

Students of literature know the epic as a long narrative poem that presents the deeds of gods or traditional heroes in a dignified manner. The eighth century B.C. saw the creation of two great Greek epics, the "Iliad" and the "Odyssey," which are attributed to Homer. The "Iliad" describes the clash of arms between Greeks and Trojans "on the ringing plains of windy Troy." The "Odyssey" relates the adventure-filled wanderings of Odysseus in his return to Greece after Troy's fall.

These epics glorify heroic valor and physical prowess. They also provide us with much detail of everyday life in ancient Greece.

The Greeks set many of their epics to music. Music helped narrators recall the wording of the epics, which tended to be extremely long pieces with dozens of verses and many names of people and places. By rhyming the lines, narrators found they could more easily remember the intricate story they had to tell.

The Greeks did not use these "story songs" as part of their worship. (Greek temples were used for sheltering gods, not religious assembly.) The use of the epic song in worship started with the Hebrews, centuries before the Greek epics were written. The earliest Hebrew worship songs arose out of a religious feeling toward God at important moments.

For instance, the first recorded appearance of story music was when Miriam, Moses' sister, sang with joy after the Jews escaped the Pharaoh's men (Exod. 15:19-21). Many of the Psalms were epics (e.g., Psa. 114, 136–137) and the prophets sometimes burst forth in epic songs (e.g., Isa. 26; Hab. 3).

The Hebrews did not apply intricate melodies to their epics. The tonal range of their songs was probably not great, and they selected rhythm instruments rather than melodic instruments. The melodies of the Psalms and other story songs were well-known in their time, and were probably sung in verses by choirs. It is clear that the Hebrews came to consider the story songs an essential part of their worship. Their music sprang from the soul of a people whose everyday life was religiously ordered.

---

stroking the strings with a plectrum, much as a guitar can be played with a pick. However, David seemed to prefer to use his hand instead (1 Sam. 16:16, 23; 18:10; 19:9). Skilled craftsmen made lyres of silver or ivory and decorated them with lavish ornamentation.

5. Psaltery. *See* "Harp."

6. Sackbut. *See* "Trigon."

7. Trigon. The Book of Daniel frequently refers to the trigon (Dan. 3:5, 7, 10, 15). The KJV incorrectly calls it the sackbut; the sackbut was not devised until several centuries after biblical times.

We do not know the exact shape and size of the trigon. The

Captive lyrists. Three captive lyrists (possibly Jews from Lachish) are conducted through a mountainous area by an Assyrian soldier armed with club and bow. The lyre made a sweet, ringing sound when its strings were plucked with a *plectrum* (a thin piece of bone or metal). This alabaster relief comes from the ruins of the palace of Sennacherib (704-681 B.C.) at Nineveh.

instrument appears to have been borrowed from the Babylonians and thus was not common among the instruments of Israel.

8. Viol. *See* "Harp."

C. Wind Instruments. Despite their limited knowledge of metal-working, the Israelites fashioned a variety of horns and other wind instruments.

1. Clarinet. The primitive clarinet was a popular instrument in Bible times. It is mentioned in Isaiah 5:12; 30:29; and Jeremiah 48:36. It is incorrectly translated as *pipe* (KJV) or *flute* (RSV) in these verses. New Testament references include Matthew 9:23; 11:17; Luke 7:32; and 1 Corinthians 14:7. The clarinet probably was not used in the temple but it was a popular instrument for banquets, weddings, or funerals.

2. Cornet. *See* "Trumpet," "Shophar," and "Rattle-Sistrum."

3. Flute. The flute (*mashrokitha*) was actually a big pipe. (The KJV uses *pipe*.) Because it was a big pipe and had a mouthpiece, it produced a sharp, penetrating sound, somewhat like an oboe. The flute was popular for secular and religious use but it was not mentioned as an instrument of the first temple orchestra. It was sometimes allowed in the second temple. Because of its penetrating sound it was used in processions (Isa. 30:29).

4. Organ. *See* "Pipe."

5. Pipe. *Pipe* usually refers to a wind instrument that was used to express wild joy or ecstatic lament. It is generally believed to have been a secular instrument, although Psalm 150:4 mentions its use in the temple for a religious celebration.

The King James Version uses the terms *organ* and *flute* instead of *pipe*.

6. Shophar. The *shophar* is best understood as a "ram's horn," as in Josh. 6:4, 6, 8, 13. The KJV often uses *trumpet, cornet,* and *horn* to render this Hebrew word (cf. 1 Chron. 15:28; 2 Chron. 15:14; Hosea 5:8). It was designed to make noise, not music, so it could not play melodies. It was used to give signals and announce special occasions, such as the transfer of the ark (2 Sam. 6). It was also used to frighten away evil spirits and gods of the enemy (Zech. 9:14-15).

7. Trumpet. The trumpet was similar to the *shophar* but was used by the priests. Trumpets were often used in pairs (Num. 10:1-10). Originally two were ordered for the temple; but the number could be increased to 120, depending upon the purpose (2 Chron. 5:12).

Trumpets were made of bones, shell or metals—bronze, copper, silver, gold—all of which produced a high, shrill sound. It is generally believed that these trumpets, like the *shophar,* could not produce sounds in various pitches, so as to make music (melody). However, they could blow legato and staccato notes and trills. Thus, they could convey complicated signals to announce assembly, battle, and ambush.

Gideon used trumpets to terrorize the enemy (Judges 7:19-20). John heard the sound of a trumpet before he received his vision of the apocalypse (Rev. 1:10). In fact, trumpets are among the prominent symbols of the Judgment (1 Cor. 15:52; 1 Thess. 4:16; Rev. 8:2).

11

WORSHIP RITUALS

The people of Israel worshipped the living God in many ways and at many different places throughout the year. It is important to see what impact their worship rituals had upon their daily lives.

First, we need to understand how the people of the Bible felt about the God they worshiped. Moses told the people of Israel, "Thou art a holy people unto the Lord thy God: the Lord thy God hath chosen thee to be a special people unto himself above all people that are upon the face of the earth" (Deut. 7:6). God chose them not because of anything they did or were, but because *He loved them* (Deut. 7:7). God showed this love in many ways. He was faithful to His covenant (v. 9); He destroyed their enemies (v. 10); He blessed them with good harvests (v. 13); and He took away their diseases (v. 15).

In response to God's actions, the Israelites were a thankful people. The Psalmist said, "It is good to give thanks unto the Lord, to sing praises unto thy name, O Most High; to show forth thy loving-kindness in the morning, and thy faithfulness every night. . ." (Psa. 92:1-2).

They stood in awe of God. As one sage observed, "The fear [awe] of the Lord is the beginning of knowledge" (Prov. 1:7). These responses were expressed in their worship. Of course, the Israelites responded to God with a whole range of thought and emotion; but these two—thankfulness and awe—seem to typify their relationship with Him.

We also need to understand how God and Israel interacted. For example, it was easy to see God in the lives of the patriarchs. He enabled Sarah to bear children at an old age (Gen. 18:9-10). He tested Abraham and spared Isaac from death (Gen. 22). He spoke with the people and they with Him

171

(Gen. 13:14-17; 15:2). But the Israelites were never allowed to see God; Moses had to hide his face from God's presence "for he was afraid to look upon God" (Exod. 3:6).

We will see how the Israelites expressed their thankfulness and awe to the heavenly Father, how they engaged in worship.

BEFORE THE TIME OF MOSES

The first clear mention of a worship act is found in Genesis 4:2-7: "And Abel was a keeper of sheep, but Cain was a tiller of the ground. And in process of time it came to pass that Cain brought of the fruit of the ground, an offering unto the Lord. And Abel, he also brought of the flock and of the fat thereof." The children of Adam and Eve recognized that God had given them "every herb" and "every beast" (Gen. 1:29-30), so they brought simple offerings to Him. We do not know precisely where and how the offerings were made. But we are told that they brought two types of offering, and that Cain's was rejected while Abel's was accepted.

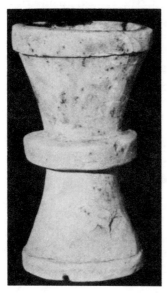

Stone altar. Found outside the gate leading into Beer-sheba, this stone altar is typical of those used in the Near East for offering sacrifices. The Israelites were supposed to offer sacrifice only at Jerusalem, but many disobeyed this law.

This brief account tells us two very important things about worship: First, God acknowledges worship. We do not know whether He had spoken to the brothers at this particular site prior to this day. But on this day God spoke (Gen. 4:6) and acted (Gen. 4:4-5) as they were worshiping. God made this time holy for them. Second, God is the focal point of worship. Scripture makes no mention of any altar or any words spoken by these men. We do not know what prayers they might have offered. But we *are* told what God did; His action was the vital part of worship.

Scripture does not tell us why Cain and Abel made offerings to God, simply that they did so "in process of time." We can suppose that they wanted to give thanks for what God had given them. They knew God had blessed them and would continue to bless them. So they were motivated not only by past events, but by their future hopes. Their sacrifices were made with dual intent: thankfulness for what God had given them and trust that He would continue to give. It is important to remember both aspects of worship and not downplay one or the other.

We cannot be sure why Abel's offering was accepted and Cain's rejected. We haven't been told of any rules regarding sacrifices at this time. The clue may appear in verse 1: "If thou doest well, shalt thou not be accepted?" In other words, Cain's faulty character may have rendered his sacrifice meaningless.

This is the first recorded instance of animal sacrifice. As time passed, the people learned that God honored and accepted their sacrificial offerings.

The patriarchs erected altars and made sacrifices wherever they settled (cf. Gen. 8:20; 12:7-8). They erected stone monuments as well. Jacob took the stone that he used as a pillow and "set it up for a pillar, and poured oil upon the top of it" (Gen. 28:18-22). He called it *Bethel,* or "God's house."

The patriarchs also designated sacred trees (e.g., Gen. 12:6; 35:4; Deut. 11:30; Josh. 24:26) and sacred wells (Gen. 16:14). These objects reminded them of what God had done at particular times in their lives.

The patriarchs built simple earthen and stone altars ("cairn altars") for the slaughter of animal offerings. In fact, the Hebrew word usually translated as *altar (mizbeach)* literally means "a place of slaughter."

There seems to have been no formal priesthood in the time of the patriarchs, yet we read of a striking encounter between Abraham and Melchizedek, a mysterious "priest of the most high God." Some scholars speculate that Melchizedek was a Canaanite king from Salem. Abraham met him after rescuing some of his captive kinsmen (Gen. 14:17-20). Because God had enabled Abraham to bring about the rescue, he responded with worshipful gratitude. Rather than building an altar or offering an animal sacrifice, Abraham offered a "tenth of everything" as sacrifice and received God's blessing through the mediator, Melchizedek. This mysterious figure is the first priest mentioned in the Bible.

Were there other priests at this time? If so, why are they not named? Perhaps the patriarchs usually acted as their own priests. They were the only ones reported to offer sacrifice to God. But if they functioned for others as clergy, that is not clearly stated.

There was spontaneity in the worship of the patriarchs. At first they left their altars uncovered and exposed to the weather; this surely affected the time of the ceremonies, since burning was a vital part of them. Also, God acted and spoke when He chose, and the patriarchs could not know in advance when God would call them to worship. Since only a handful of people worshiped at one time, there was no need for a scheduled worship time.

IN THE TIME OF MOSES

Moses inaugurated a new period in Israel's worship practices—a period that extended far beyond the lifetime of Moses. It began as Moses led the people of Israel out from Egypt (1446 B.C.), but Moses' direct influence on worship practice extended throughout Jewish history. For practical reasons, in this section let us focus on Moses' influence until

Model of tabernacle. This model constructed by Dr. Conrad Schick shows the tabernacle, a movable tent sanctuary made according to instructions that God gave to Moses on Mount Sinai. One special compartment of the tabernacle, called the "holy of holies," was revered as the place where God dwelled. Only the high priest could enter this place, and he did so only one day of the year—on the Day of Atonement.

the time of the judges (which ended in 1043 B.C. with the naming of Saul as Israel's first king). During the time of the judges, God's people still worshiped in tents or tabernacles. But when David was king, plans were made for construction of a temple; our next section deals with that.

A. The Worship Site. We have already mentioned that God sanctioned the use of earthen and stone altars (Exod. 20:24-26). In the days of Moses, God also sanctioned a new kind of worship site. When the great lawgiver climbed to the top of Mount Sinai, he received much more than the Ten Commandments. Among other things, he received a plan for an enclosed worship site, with an altar housed in a cloth tent. It is difficult to construct a picture of this new site. Many artists have drawn their impressions, based upon the Bible's descriptions; but there is no complete agreement on the plan of the tabernacle.

Yet we know that this worship site was distinctly different from the altars erected under the open sky. For one thing, it was much more elaborate. A description of the altar itself is found in Exodus 27:1-3: "Thou shalt make an altar of shittim wood, five cubits long, and five cubits broad; the altar shall be foursquare: and the height thereof shall be three cubits. And

Model of the ark of the covenant. The ark was a rectangular box of acacia wood that contained the tables of the Ten Commandments, a pot of manna, and Aaron's rod. The lid, or "mercy seat," was a gold plate surrounded by golden cherubim with outstretched wings. The ark was the symbol of God's presence among His people.

thou shalt make the horns of it upon the four corners thereof: his horns shall be of the same: and thou shalt overlay it with brass. And thou shalt make his pans to receive his ashes, and his shovels, and his basins, and his fleshhooks, and his firepans: all the vessels thereof thou shalt make of brass."

Not only were the materials different from the first altars, but the tools required to make it and the accompanying utensils were different (cf. Exod. 20:25). There is good evidence that Israel used both kinds of altars—those outdoors and the one in the tabernacle—during this time. Eventually, a more permanent, central altar was erected in the tabernacle.

Scripture also describes the tent that now covered the altar: "And Moses took the tabernacle, and pitched it without the camp, afar off from the camp, and called it the tabernacle of the congregation. And it came to pass, that everyone which sought the Lord went out unto the tabernacle of the congregation, which was without the camp. And it came to pass, when Moses went out unto the tabernacle, that all the people rose up, and stood every man at his tent door, and looked after Moses, until he was gone into the tabernacle. And it came to pass, as Moses entered into the tabernacle, the cloudy pillar descended, and stood at the door of the tabernacle, and the Lord talked with Moses" (Exod. 33:7-10). The tent is described again in Exodus 26. With such a detailed description, it may seem easy to illustrate how the tent looked. But it isn't. It would be just as challenging to picture an automobile engine if we had only a verbal blueprint and had never actually seen one.

Moses spoke with God in this tent. Although Scripture does not say that Moses offered sacrifices in the tent (cf. Exod. 33:7-10), we may assume that he did so, since the altar was there. Moses was seeking the Lord. The people knew God was meeting with Moses because the "cloudy pillar" stood before the tent. This was a familiar sign of God's presence.

Moses and his servant Joshua went into the tent alone while the other people stood by and waited. After Moses first worshiped in the tent, he returned to the mountain to receive new tables of Law. He then came down to relay God's message to His people.

In a sense, Moses was a "go-between" for God and the Israelites. He was not a formal priest, but God did single him out as His leader-messenger. We can see the beginnings of priesthood here; but Moses himself was not actually called a priest until centuries later (cf. Psa. 99:6).

B. The Priesthood. At this point in Israel's history, an ordained priesthood came into being. According to God's command (Exod. 28:1), Moses consecrated his brother Aaron and Aaron's sons as priests. These men came from the tribe of Levi. From this point until intertestamental times, the official priesthood belonged to the Levites.

Moses made a distinction between Aaron and his sons, for he anointed Aaron as the "high priest among his brethren" (Lev. 21:10). He distinguished Aaron's office by giving him

Stairway to Hulda Gates. Scholars believe that pilgrims may have sung the Songs of Ascent (Psa. 120–134) as they made their journeys to sites hallowed in Israelite tradition. This wide stairway, uncovered south of the temple mount and leading to the Hulda Gates in Jerusalem, is probably the stairway that pilgrims ascended on their way to the inner courts of the temple.

special robes (Exod. 28:4, 6-39; Lev. 8:7-9). Upon Aaron's death, the robes and the office were transferred to Eleazar, his eldest son (Num. 20:25-28).

The high priest's most important function was to preside at the annual Day of Atonement. On that day, the high priest could enter the holy of holies of the tabernacle and sprinkle the mercy seat with the blood of sin offerings. By doing this, he atoned for his wrongs, for those of his family, and those of all the people of Israel (Lev. 16:1-25). The high priest also had to sprinkle the blood from the sin offerings before the veil of the sanctuary and on the horns of the altar (Lev. 4:3-21).

As the spiritual head of Israel, the high priest had to attain a greater degree of ceremonial purity than did the ordinary priests. Leviticus 21:10-15 outlines requirements for purity of the high priest. Any sin he might commit was a blight upon the entire people of Israel. He had to atone for such a sin with a specially prescribed offering (Lev. 4:3-12).

The high priest also offered the daily meal offering (Lev. 6:19-22) and participated in the general duties of the priesthood (Exod. 27:21). These duties were many. Priests presided over all sacrifices and feasts. They served as medical advisors to the community (Lev. 13:15), and they were administrators of justice (Deut. 17:8-9; 21:5; Num. 5:11-13). Only they could give a blessing in the name of God (Num. 6:22-27) and blow the trumpets that summoned the people to war or feast (Num. 10:1-10).

Levites served as priests either from age 30 to 50 (Num. 4:39) or from age 25 to 50 (Num. 3:23-26). After age 50, they were only allowed to assist their fellow priests.

The people's tithe provided food and clothing for the priests (Lev. 32-33); a tenth of the tithe was given to the priests (Num. 18:21, 24-32). Since the tribe of Levi possessed no territory, 48 cities and surrounding pastures were given to them (Num. 35:1-8).

C. The Sacrificial System. The Bible contains many of Moses' regulations for sacrifice, but Leviticus 1–7 is wholly dedicated to the ritual. Many scholars regard this section as a kind of "handbook for sacrifice." It describes 5 types of sacrifice: burnt offerings, cereal offerings, peace offerings, sin offerings, and trespass offerings.

1. Burnt Offerings. This type of sacrifice was wholly burnt. None of it is eaten by anyone; the fire consumed it all. In fact, the fire was never extinguished: "The fire shall ever be burning upon the altar; it shall never go out" (Lev. 6:13).

The worshiper brought a male animal—a bull, lamb, goat, pigeon, or turtledove (depending largely upon the worshiper's wealth)—to the door of the tent or temple. The animal had to be without blemish. The worshiper then placed his hands upon the animal's head and it was "accepted for him to make atonement for him" (Lev. 1:4). The laying of hands was a ceremonial act whereby the worshiper blessed or prepared the sacrificial animal. The animal was then killed at the door. Immediately, the priest collected the animal's blood and sprinkled it about the altar. (Priests never drank the blood.) Next, the priest quartered the animal, offered its head and fat on the altar, then washed the legs and entrails in water and offered them. Any remains might be cast aside into the ashes. (For example, this was done with a bird's feathers.)

Besides placing the animal on the altar, the priests were responsible to maintain the fire. They could not permit the ashes to build up in the bottom of the altar, but put them beside the altar at various times. Later, they took the ashes outside the camp or city "unto a clean place." They changed their clothes to do this.

Later in Israel's history, the burnt offering became a continually offered sacrifice: "This is the offering made by fire which ye shall offer unto the Lord; two lambs of the first year without spot day by day, for a continued burnt offering" (Num. 28:3). As this passage indicates, two animals were sacrificed each day, one at morning and one at evening. This was done to atone the people's sins against the Lord (Lev. 6:2). The burning symbolized the nation's desire to rid itself of these sinful acts against God.

2.   Cereal Offerings. The Israelites sacrificed cereals or vegetable produce in addition to animals. These crops might have been offered independently of the burnt offerings, or along with them. The Hebrew word for "oblation" *(minha)* sometimes refers to these cereal offerings; at other times, *minha* referred to other types of sacrifice.

Leviticus 2 mentions 4 kinds of cereal offerings and gives cooking instructions for each. A worshiper could offer dough from wheat flour that has been baked in an oven, cooked on a griddle, fried in a pan, or roasted to make bread. (The last method was used for the offerings of first fruits.) All cereal offerings were made with oil and salt; no honey or leaven could be used. Oil and salt would not spoil, while honey and leaven would. In addition to these cooked ingredients, the worshiper was to bring a portion of incense (frankincense). He might also bring portions of the uncooked materials (raw grains, salt, and oil) with the offering.

Worshipers brought cereal offerings to one of two priests, who took it to the altar and threw a "memorial portion" (either of the bread, cake, wafer, or uncooked ingredients) on

When Sacrifice Stopped

Judea Capta—"Judea is captured"—read the coins minted by the Romans in commemoration of their victory in A.D. 70. Thousands of Jews died in battle; thousands more were taken into slavery; many others chose to leave the country. Their center of worship, the temple, was burned to the ground and the capital of Judaism had fallen.

The Roman emperors redirected the temple tax, formerly collected from all Jews, to the temple of Jupiter Capitolinus in Rome. Grieving Jews abstained from eating meat and wine, formerly temple staples; they felt it wrong to enjoy what could no longer be offered to God.

With the end of temple worship, the priesthood began to decline. Although the priests could still receive heave offerings and tithes, their revenues were greatly reduced. This loss of income, plus the loss of their temple function, resulted in a loss of influence and authority.

Deuteronomy forbade altars and sacrifices outside the chosen place, Jerusalem. But this was not the first time the Jews had been deprived of their temple and sacrifical worship; during the Exile, the people had assembled regularly to read the Scriptures and to discuss their meaning. These *synagogues* (Greek, "assemblies") again became vital to Judaism after the temple was destroyed.

Jewish people met at the synagogue to pray, sing, and study the Torah. The chief function of the synagogue was to foster understanding and proper observance of the Jewish law. In effect, it became the seat of a spiritual government which ordered and disciplined the lives of the people.

After the destruction of the temple, the sages who interpreted the Law came to be called *tannaim*, and those who were authorized as leaders were given the title *rabbi*, or "doctor of the law." Sages interpreted the laws found in the Pentateuch as well as the

traditional, oral laws called the *halakoth*. They were chiefly concerned with how these laws should effect the lives of the people. Followers of the great sage Shammai were noted for their conservative interpretations, while followers of the sage Hillel adhered to more liberal interpretations.

Jabneh (modern Jamnia) on the western Judean plains soon became the center of Jewish learning. During the war with Rome, the sage Johanan ben Zakkai was smuggled out of Jerusalem in a coffin. He made his way to the Roman camp, where he asked Roman authorities to allow him and his disciples to settle the coastal city of Jabneh and to establish an academy there. Johanan rightly perceived that the only important victory to be secured in the war against Rome was the survival of Judaism. If need be, a vitalized tradition could become a "portable homeland" for the Jews. Jabneh became the new center of that tradition.

After the Bar-Kochba revolt in A.D. 135, the center of Jewish studies was moved to Usha in Galilee, near modern Haifa. Here the sages began the assembling and codifying of the halakoth in a document that came to be called *Mishna*.

The sages disagreed as to how the halakoth should be organized. One group thought it should follow the order of the biblical verses to which they referred. Another group, headed by Rabbi Akiba ben Joseph, held out for arranging the sayings by subject matter, the way that was eventually followed.

The task of assembling the Mishna was not completed until the early part of the third century. The Mishna and the *Gemara* (a commentary on the Mishna), comprise the chief parts of the Jewish sacred book called the *Talmud*. This comprehensive compilation of Jewish manners, customs, beliefs, and teachings is still revered and studied by Jewish scholars.

the fire. He did the same with all the incense. The priest ate the remainder; but if the priest himself was making a cereal offering, he burned the entire sacrifice.

The cereal offering's purpose appears to have been similar to that of the burnt offering—except in case of the "corn" offering, which was linked to the offering of first fruits (Lev. 2:14). The offering of first fruits seems to have been intended to sanctify the entire crop. The "corn" offering substituted for the rest of the crop—emphasizing that all of the crop was holy unto the Lord.

3. Peace Offerings. A ritual meal called the "peace offering" was shared with God, the priests, and sometimes other worshipers. It involved male or female oxen, sheep, or goats. The procedure was nearly identical to that of the burnt offering up to the point of the actual burning. In this case, the beast's blood was collected and poured around the edges of the altar. The fat and entrails were burned. Then the remainder was eaten by the priests and (if the offering was voluntary) by the worshipers themselves. This sacrifice expressed the worshiper's desire to give thanks or praise to God. Sometimes, he was required to do this; at other times he might do so voluntarily.

The required offerings made included unleavened cakes. The priests had to eat all but the memorial portion of the cakes and the remainder of the animal on the same day the sacrifice was made.

When the offering was voluntary, the regulations were not so strict. The worshipers did not need to bring cakes and could eat for two days, not one. The priest's portion was limited to the breast and right thigh of the animal, while anyone who was ceremonially clean could eat of the rest.

Jacob and Laban offered this kind of sacrifice when they made a treaty (Gen. 31:43ff.). Some scholars call this a "vow offering." "Thank offerings" and "free-will offerings" followed the same general pattern. Saul's sacrifice (1 Sam 13:8ff.) fell into the latter category; although he "forced himself" to do it, he certainly was not required to do it. (In fact, Samuel chastised him, saying that it was illegal.) The vow and thank offerings were required, while free-will offerings were voluntary.

4. Sin Offerings. Sacrifices for sin "paid off" or *expiated* a worshiper's ritual faults against the Lord. These were unintentional faults. "And the Lord spoke unto Moses, saying, Speak unto the children of Israel, saying, If a soul shall sin *through ignorance* against any of the commandments of the Lord concerning things which ought not to be done, and shall do against any of them" (Lev. 4:1-2, italics added). Moses instructed various people to offer different sacrifices in these cases:

Sins of the high priest were atoned with the offering of a bull. The blood was not poured on the altar, but sprinkled from the finger of the high priest 7 times on the altar. The fat from the entrails was burned next. The remainder was burned, not eaten, outside the camp or city "unto a clean place, where the ashes are poured out."

Sins of leaders in the community are atoned with the offerings of a male goat. The blood was sprinkled only once, then the remainder was poured around the altar as in the burnt offering.

Jezebel's Idolatry

Jezebel, daughter of King Ethbaal of Sidon, was raised in Sidon, a commercial city on the coast of the Mediterranean Sea. Sidon was considered to be a center of vice and ungodliness. When Jezebel married King Ahab of Israel, she moved to Jezreel, a city that served Jehovah. Jezebel soon decided to turn Jezreel into a city similar to her native town.

Jezebel tried to convince her husband to begin serving the golden calf, under the pretense that such worship would really be a service to Jehovah. Actually, the calf was a central idol in the worship of Baal, a sun-god who was important to ancient Phoenicians. Because Baal was believed to have power over crops, flocks, and the fertility of farm families, the golden calf was often linked with him. As the worship of Baal spread to countries bordering Phoenicia, more peoples adopted the religion's lascivious rites, which included human sacrifice, self-torture, and kissing the image. The practices of the Baal cult offended pious Jews, but because King Ahab was easily manipulated by Jezebel, beautiful temples honoring Baal were soon erected throughout Israel.

The priests of Jehovah opposed Jezebel; many of them were murdered. Even the great prophet Elijah fled from her wrath (1 Kings 18:4-19).

In her effort to erase the mark of Jehovah throughout Israel, Jezebel became the first female religious persecutor in Bible history. She so effectively injected the poison of idolatry into the veins of Israel that the nation suffered.

Elijah said, "The dogs shall eat Jezebel by the wall of Jezreel" (1 Kings 21:23). This prophesy came true; only Jezebel's skull, feet, and the palms of her hands were left to bury (2 Kings 9:36-37).

The hearts of the Israelites must have been ripe for idolatry, or Jezebel would not have been able to so pervert their religion. King Ahab committed a grave sin against God by marrying her, because Jezebel worshiped Baal (1 Kings 21:25-26).

Sins of private individuals were atoned with female animals: goats, lambs, turtledoves, or pigeons. If a person could not afford one of those, an offering of grain was acceptable. The procedure for offering the grain was the same as in the cereal offerings.

It would be impossible to name all the ways a person might commit an unintentional sin against God. Some had moral implications. Others, like those of lepers (cf. Luke 5:22ff.), were purely ceremonial. Another example of sacrifice for a ceremonial fault would be the offering that a woman made after she gave birth, in order to recover her ceremonial cleanliness (Lev. 12). Offerings for the nation and for the high priest covered all these in a collective way. On the Day of Atonement *(Yom Kippur),* the high priest sprinkled blood over the ark of the covenant itself. This was the ultimate ritual of atonement.

5. Trespass Offerings. The trespass offering was similar to the sin offering, and many scholars include it in the former category. It differed only in that the trespass offering was an offering of money. This sacrifice was made for sins of ignorance, connected with fraud. For example, if the worshiper had unwittingly cheated another of money or property, his sacrifice must be equal to the value of the amount taken, plus one-fifth. He offered this amount to the priest, then made a similar restitution to the former property owner. Therefore he repaid twice the amount he had taken plus 40 percent (Lev. 6:5-6).

All of these sacrifices related directly to either *expiation* (guilt removal) or *propitiation* (keeping God's favor). They remind us again of the two strong emotions in all of worship: awe and thankfulness.

D. The Ritual Year. The people of Israel worshiped God at times He chose or whenever they "sought him." But under Moses' leadership, worship became mandatory at certain times of the year. The people began observing the Sabbath and other appointed worship days.

The most important events on the ritual calendar were the three great pilgrim feasts—Passover, the Feast of Weeks (Pentecost), and the Feast of Tabernacles (or Booths). On each of these occasions, the Israelite males journeyed to the central place of worship to offer sacrifices to God.

1. The Sabbath. There seems to have been no observance of a special day of rest among Hebrews before the time of Moses. The first mention of the Sabbath is in Exodus 16:23, when the Hebrews camped in the Wilderness of Sin before they received the Ten Commandments. There God instructed them to observe the Sabbath every 7 days, in honor of His work of creation (Exod. 20:8-11; cf. Gen. 2:1-3) and Israel's release from bondage (Deut. 5:12-15; cf. Exod. 32:12). The Sabbath separated the Israelites from work and all other ordinary activity (Exod. 35:2-3); thus it reminded them of Israel's separation from the nations around them, and of their relation to God as a covenant people.

A great deal of legal material in the first five books of the Bible concerns the keeping of the Sabbath. Breaking the Sabbath was like breaking Israel's covenant with God; thus it

The Sacred Rock. Now in the center of the Mosque of Omar (completed A.D. 691), this rock is located on the site of Solomon's and Herod's temples. Many believe the rock once formed the base of the Jewish altar. The spot is also sacred to the Muslims, who believe that Muhammed ascended into heaven from this point.

was punishable by death (Num. 15:32-36). Two lambs were sacrificed on the Sabbath, as opposed to one lamb on other days (Num. 28:9, 19). Twelve cakes of showbread (representing the 12 tribes of Israel) were presented in the tabernacle on the Sabbath (Lev. 24:5-8).

2. Passover and the Feast of Unleavened Bread. During Israel's great pilgrim feasts, all males were required to appear before the sanctuary of the Lord (Deut. 16:16). The first and most important of these was the feast of *Passover*. It combined two observances that originally were separate: *Passover,* the night celebrated in memory of the death angel's passing over the Hebrew households in Egypt, and *the Feast of Unleavened Bread,* which commemorated the first 7 days of the Exodus itself. The two celebrations were closely intertwined. For example, leaven had to be removed from the house before the slaying of the Passover lamb (Deut. 16:4). Therefore, the Passover meal itself was one of unleavened bread (Exod. 12:8). Eventually, the people of Israel merged the two celebrations into one.

This great festival began on the evening of the fourteenth day of Abib (which would have been considered the beginning of the fifteenth day). The lamb or kid was slain just prior to sunset (Exod. 12:6; Deut. 16:6) and was roasted whole and eaten with unleavened bread and bitter herbs. The ceremony was full of symbolism: The blood of the animal symbolized the cleansing of sins. Bitter herbs represented the bitterness of bondage in Egypt. And the unleavened bread was a symbol of purity.

Entire families participated in the Passover supper. If the family was small, neighbors joined them until there were enough to eat the entire lamb (Exod. 12:4). The head of the household recited Israel's history during the meal.

The first and seventh days of the celebration were kept as Sabbaths: There was no work and the people came together for a holy gathering (Exod. 12:16; Lev. 23:7; Num. 28:18, 25). On the second day of the festival, a priest waved a sheaf of first-ripe barley before the Lord to consecrate the beginning harvest. In addition to the regular sacrifices in the sanctuary, the priests daily sacrificed two bullocks, one ram, and seven lambs as a burnt offering and a male goat as a sin offering (Lev. 23:8; Num. 28:19-23).

3. The Feast of Weeks (Pentecost). This festival was observed 50 days after the offering of the barley sheaf at the Feast of Unleavened Bread. It marked the end of the harvest and the beginning of the seasonal offering of first fruits (Exod. 23:16; Lev. 23:15-21; Num. 28:26-31; Deut. 16:9-12). This one-day festival was observed as a Sabbath with a holy gathering at the tabernacle. Two loaves of unleavened bread were offered, along with 10 proper animals for a burnt offering, a male goat for a sin offering, and two yearling male lambs for a peace offering. Priests urged the people to remember the needy at this festival (Deut. 16:11-12), as they were to do at all pilgrim festivals.

4. The Feast of Tabernacles (Booths). This festival commemorated Israel's wandering in the wilderness. It took its name from the fact that the Israelites lived in tents or arbors during the celebration (Lev. 23:40-42). The festival began on the fifteenth day of the seventh month (Tishri), and lasted for seven days. It fell at the end of the harvest season—thus a third name for the festival, the "Feast of Ingathering" (Exod. 23:16; 34:22; Lev. 23:39; Deut. 16:13-15). The priest offered a special burnt offering of 70 bullocks during the week. Two rams and 14 lambs were the daily burnt offering, and a male goat the daily sin offering (Num. 29:12-34).

Every seventh year, when there was no harvest because of the sabbatical year, the Law of Moses was read publicly during the feast. At a later time, another day was added to the Feast of Booths for this purpose. It was known as the *Simhath Torah* ("Joy of the Law"), in honor of the Law.

Ritual bath. Priests washed various cult objects in this basin to achieve ceremonial purity. The early Hebrews considered cleanliness to be both a physical and a moral attribute. Diseased people and the objects they touched were considered unclean (Lev. 15:22).

5. The Day of Atonement. The Law of Moses required only one fast—the Day of Atonement (Exod. 30:10; Lev. 16; 23:31-32; 25:9; Num. 29:7-11). This day fell on the tenth day of Tishri, just before the Feast of Booths.

The day was set aside for the cleansing of sins. It was observed by abstaining from work, fasting, and attending a holy gathering. The high priest replaced his elaborate robes with a simple white linen garment and offered a sin offering for himself, his household, and the entire nation of Israel.

One interesting feature of the day's observance was that the high priest symbolically transferred the sins of the people onto a goat, or *scapegoat.* The high priest laid his hands on the head of the goat and confessed the people's sins. Then the goat was led away into the wilderness, where it was abandoned to die. (In later years, an attendant led the goat out of Jerusalem and pushed it off one of the cliffs surrounding the city.) This act ended the rites of the Day of Atonement. The people, free of sin, danced and rejoiced (cf. Psa. 103:12).

FROM THE MONARCHY TO EXILE

Israel's worship patterns changed noticeably from the time of the monarchy (which began when Saul became king in 1043 B.C.) until the time of the Exile (which began when the Babylonians seized Judah in 586 B.C.).

Before this time, the people of Israel worshiped God at many different places; under the kings, their worship would be focused on a central place of sacrifice. Before, a person could make an offering on the spur of the moment; now, he had to follow the procedures established by the Law of Moses.

A. The Temple. Israel's first king, Saul, seemed to be confused about the proper way of worship. Faced with sure defeat at the hands of the Philistines, he reverted to the old ways. He built an altar on the spot of his encampment and asked for God's help. Samuel arrived shortly afterward to remind him of the Lord's commandment not to worship at "every place" (1 Sam. 13:8-14; cf. Deut. 12:13).

Under the leadership of David, Israel became stronger and wealthier as a nation. After he built a great palace of cedar, it seemed to him wrong that he lived "in a house of cedar, but the ark of God dwelleth within curtains" (2 Sam. 7:2). Therefore, with the prophet Nathan's blessing, David gathered materials and purchased the site for a temple, a house of God (2 Sam 24:18-25; 1 Chron. 22:3). However, it was not for him to build the temple (1 Chron. 22:6-19), but for his son Solomon.

First Kings 6–7 and 2 Chronicles 3–4 contain descriptions of the temple. There is a remarkable similarity between Solomon's temple and the plans for the tabernacle (Exod. 25–28). For example, each had two chambers or courts. The altars in the temple were bronze with utensils similar to the tabernacle's. Most portrayals of the temple include steps up to a porch with two columns on either side of a doorway. Inside the smaller chamber was the ark of the covenant. A hallway for storing the national treasure surrounded the whole building.

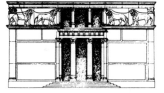

Diagram of temple at Araq-el-Emir. This reconstruction of a Jewish temple built by the Maccabeans under John Hyrcanus is based on findings from excavations of the site. The facade of the building, erected early in the second century B.C., was decorated with colossal figures of lions in relief. The rectangular interior featured four corner rooms, one of which was a staircase tower.

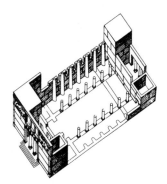

In later days, Solomon's temple was desecrated in various ways by unfaithful Jewish kings (cf. 1 Kings 14:26; 2 Kings 12:4-15; 16:8; 18:15-16; 21:4; 23:1-12). It was finally destroyed by Nebuchadnezzar in 586 B.C.

B. The Priests, Prophets, and Kings. A formal priesthood developed among the tribe of Levi in the time of Moses. However, under the monarchy there were examples of non-Levitical priests (2 Sam. 8:17; 20:26; 1 Kings 4:5). First Kings 12:31 tells us that Jeroboam, the first king of the northern kingdom of Israel, set up his own priesthood: "Priests . . . which were not of the sons of Levi."

Priestly assignments were very specialized during the monarchy. For example, one group had charge of the altar, and another of the lamp oil.

But the people recognized that God had spokesmen other than the priests. When the people wanted a king, they went to Samuel, *the prophet.* What role did prophets play in Israel's worship?

We know that prophets gave advice to kings (1 Kings 22), but they also spoke to the people at the sanctuaries. There was actually a formal "prophet-hood," much like there was a distinct priesthood; Amos tells us this by denying that he belongs to it (Amos 7:14). The two groups—priests and prophets—had different purposes and functions. For instance, the Bible does not speak very often about prophets in worship; it speaks more often about their criticism of the worship practices.

The king also played an important role in Israel's worship; some say he had the most important part of all. When he interacted with God, the whole nation felt the impact (2 Sam. 21:1). The high priest anointed the king to signify that God had chosen him for his royal task (cf. 1 Sam. 10:1). As the anointed representative of the people, the king had to make sacrifices (1 Kings 8; 2 Sam. 24:25). He gathered temple materials and ordered the construction. In the end, he had the power to affect everything Israel did concerning worship. Some of the later kings polluted temple activities with foreign rituals and idols. But others forced a return to the proper ways of worship.

The people's understanding of sacrifice was challenged during this period. Notice these words from the prophet Micah: "Wherewith shall I come before the Lord, and bow myself before the high God? shall I come before him with burnt offerings, with calves a year old? Will the Lord be pleased with thousands of rams, or with ten thousands of rivers of oil? shall I give my firstborn for my transgression, the fruit of my body for the sin of my soul?" (Mic. 6:6-7). The Israelites had to realize that motive is more important than the act of sacrifice itself. They needed to see that the Lord does not require great sacrifices for their own sakes, but justice, love, and kindness (Mic. 6:8). This distinction had far-reaching effects.

Not every animal slaughter was now considered to be sacrificial. The people could kill and eat as much as they desired; but they could not eat the tithe of grain, firstlings, or any other sacrifice. They began to consider some acts of slaughter to be sacred, while some were secular.

C. Feasts. The primary festivals of this period were still the Feast of Weeks, of Unleavened Bread (Passover), and of Booths. Attendance was still required, but they were all held in Jerusalem. (Earlier, they were held wherever the ark of the covenant was located.)

Generally, worship during the monarchy was done in an atmosphere of rejoicing. There was music, shouting, and dancing. But worship was also characterized by prayers, vows, vigils, promises, sacred meals, and ritual washings.

Foreign influences began to creep into Israel's worship and the prophets loudly denounced these. Amos cried out against ritual law breaking (Amos 2:8), ritual prostitution (Amos 2:4), and worship that was not accompanied by repentance (Amos 4:4-6). He said that God detested Israel's feasts (Amos 5:21-24). The prophets also denounced idolatry in Israel's worship (2 Kings 18:4; Isa. 2:8, 20; Hos. 8:4-6; 13:1-2). Even the temple itself—its furnishings, symbolisms, and patterns of worship—showed Canaanite, Phoenician, and Egyptian influences.

The reform under King Josiah (639–608 B.C.) abolished local shrines and did away with local priestly families. All sacrifice was done in Jerusalem once again. Josiah suppressed the local cults and all rites of idolatry (2 Kings 23:4-25). After his death, however, Judah returned to "that which was evil in the sight of the Lord" (2 Kings 23:32, 37).

THE EXILE AND THE INTERTESTAMENTAL PERIOD

In 586 B.C., Nebuchadnezzar plundered Jerusalem and destroyed the holy temple Solomon had built. Now the Israelites could not worship as they had; they were forced to change. This period of Exile began what we might call the "later years" of Israel's worship.

The Bible says little about what happened at the site of the temple while the Jews were exiled. Ezekiel's "temple" was probably a vision. But Cyrus of Persia ordered the Israelites "to build [God] a house in Jerusalem" (Ezra 1:2). Cyrus also gave them back the holy vessels of gold and silver that Nebuchadnezzar had taken as booty (Ezra 5:14).

In many ways, then, the second temple would be like Solomon's. But the ark of the covenant was permanently lost during the Babylonian invasion. Only a small group of Israelites restored the temple, so capital and labor were minimal. The new building was smaller and less ornate than Solomon's had been. Yet it was styled after Moses' descriptions in Exodus 25–28.

Apparently all Jewish worship was centralized at the new temple. The Mishna tells us that the Psalms were in great use at this time. Psalms of ascents (Psa. 120–134) were used at the Feast of Booths, and the Hallel Psalms (113–118; 136) were used at all the great festivals.

The Jews felt they were under the burden of God's wrath and judgment. To make amends, they began making their offerings and sacrifices once again.

The Levites were among the first to return to Judah: "Then rose up the chief of the fathers of Judah and Benjamin, and the priests, and the Levites, with all them whose spirit God had raised, to go up to build the house for the Lord which is in Jerusalem" (Ezra 1:5). Notice that the Scriptures say "priests and Levites," as if the two were no longer synonymous. Not all Levites were now considered priests—only those who were descendants of Aaron. During the years of the monarchy other branches of the tribe of Levi had been accepted as priests. But following the Exile, all those who claimed to be priests had to prove their descent from Aaron before they were admitted (Ezra 2:61-63; Neh. 7:63-65).

Other temple personnel who returned were the singers, gatekeepers or porters, temple servants *(Nethinim)*, and the sons of Solomon's servants (Ezra 2:41-58; cf. 7:24; Neh. 7:44-60). Chronicles refers to the singers and gatekeepers as "Levites," but they were of foreign origin. They were descendants of war captives who had assisted the Levites in Solomon's temple. In Nehemiah's time these people pledged themselves "to walk in God's law" and not to marry foreigners (Neh. 10:28-30).

One very important change took place in this period after the Exile. Leviticus 10:10-11 gave the priests responsibility for both moral instruction and ceremonial matters, but the priest's teaching role seemed to disappear after the Exile. Only one mention of a priestly teaching occurs after the Exile (Hag. 2:10-13). Indeed, the prophet Malachi complained that

Samaritan sacrifice. The Samaritans still make sacrifices in accordance with the law of Moses, much as their ancestors did. Here lambs are offered on Mount Gerizim in celebration of the Passover.

the priests of his time failed in this important respect (Mal. 2:7-8). Levites other than the priests instructed the people concerning the Law (Neh. 8:7). The high priest became a king-like entity, combining functions of both religion and state.

The joyous atmosphere of the earlier rituals gave way to one of great seriousness and remorse. The ritual feasts had been primarily social meals; now they became awe-inspiring periods of introspection. After the Exile, the Israelites were seeking to learn how they could be more obedient to God's covenant.

One new and more joyous festival—the feast of Purim—was added to the ceremonial observances during this period. This festival was held on Adar 14-15 to commemorate the Jews' deliverance from Haman while they lived under Persian rule. Since the time of the Exile, Jews have observed this feast in recognition of God's continued deliverance of His people.

The Purim observance followed a fixed form. Adar 13 was a day of fasting. On the evening of that day (which is the beginning of the fourteenth day), the Jews assembled for a service in their synagogues. Following the service, the Book of Esther was read.

When the name of Haman was read, the people cried, "Let his name be blotted out," or "The name of the wicked shall rot." The names of Haman's sons were all read in one breath, to emphasize the fact that they were all hanged at the same time.

The next morning the people again went to the synagogue to finish the formal religious observance. The rest of the day was a time for merrymaking. As in other festival observances, the rich were called on to provide for the poor.

In 333 B.C., Alexander the Great began his conquest of Syria, the Middle East, and Egypt. After his death in 323 B.C., his generals divided the lands among themselves. After many years of political turmoil, a line of Syrian kings known as the Seleucids gained control of Palestine. The Seleucid ruler named Antiochus IV enforced his will upon the Jews by forbidding them to engage in sacrifices, rites, feasts, and worship of any kind.

In 167 B.C., a Syrian officer brought an unnamed Jew to the temple and forced him to make a sacrifice to Zeus. A priest named Mattathias witnessed the event. He slew them both, called for all faithful Jews to follow him, and fled for the hills outside Jerusalem. There he and his sons organized for war against the Seleucids. They swept over Jerusalem, defeated the Syrian army, and secured the city. The Syrian leaders were forced to repeal their ordinances against worship in Israel. Now the temple could be cleansed and true worship could resume. (The biblical account of this period in Israel's history can be found in the deuterocanonical books of 1 and 2 Maccabees.) Modern Jews remember this great event at the Feast of Dedication or Hanukkah. Jesus Himself was in Jerusalem at the time of a Hanukkah celebration near the end of His earthly ministry (John 10:22). This 8-day feast is celebrated on the twenty-fifth of the month. Chislev, also known as the Feast of Lights, is marked by the lighting of 8 candles—one on each day of the feast. The celebration features the singing of the Hallel Psalms and is somewhat similar to the Feast of Booths.

Under the Maccabees, the Jews worshiped in a nationalistic manner. Their hopes for a God-ruled earth brought new emphasis to their worship, such as the use of apocalyptic literature. Prophecy gradually diminished as apocalyptic took its place. One apocalyptic writer expressed his hopes for an earthly kingdom of God in this fashion: "And now, O Lord, behold, these heathen, which have ever been reputed as nothing, have begun to be lords over us, and to devour us. But we thy people, whom thou hast called thy firstborn, thy only begotten, and thy fervent lover, are given into their hands. If the world now is made for our sakes, why do we not possess an inheritance with the world? how long shall this endure?" (2 Esdras 6:57-59). During this period, however, the seer or apocalyptist spoke for God. He spoke of demons and angels, dark and light, evil and good. He predicted the final triumph of the nation of Israel. This hope flowed as the undercurrent of Jewish worship.

One other feature of worship that became more prominent in this period was the study of the Law. It was primarily a priestly duty, on which the Hasidim (Pharisees) concentrated. They produced many new teachings and doctrines in the process, notably the doctrine of the resurrection of dead.

THE NEW TESTAMENT ERA

In 47 B.C., Julius Caesar selected Herod Antipater, a Jew of Idumea (the area south of Judea), to be governor of Judea. His son, Herod the Great, inherited the position and called himself "king of the Jews." Realizing the history of unrest among the people, Herod wanted to gain their favor and faith in some way. To do this, he announced the building of a third temple at Jerusalem. Priests specially trained in construction skills did much of the work to make sure the new building followed Moses' floor plan. Most of the construction was completed in about 10 years (*ca.* 20–10 B.C.), but not all was finished until about A.D. 60. (In fact, some scholars feel the new temple had not been completed at the time Jerusalem fell to the Roman general Pompey in A.D. 63.) Most worship activities occurred here.

Yet during the persecutions and exiles of Israel, many Jews found themselves too far from Jerusalem to worship there. Did this mean that they were not able to worship at all? By no means! Rather they instituted the custom of local synagogue worship. Although the Old Testament uses the word *synagogue* only once (Psa. 74:8), many of these informal worship places surely existed during the Exile. The New Testament mentions them often (e.g., Matt. 4:23; 23:6; Acts 6:9), but gives us little descriptive information about them. We do know something of the early synagogues from rabbinic sources. We also know that the Law was studied and pronounced there: "For Moses of old time hath in every city them that preach him, being read in the synagogues every sabbath day" (Acts 15:21). Many prayers were recited in synagogue worship (Matt. 6:5). Sources outside the Bible tell us that the synagogue worship services consisted of an invocational prayer, other prayers and benedictions, the reading of the Law of Moses, the reading of

Gerizim vs. Jerusalem

"The woman saith unto Him, Sir, I perceive that thou art a prophet. Our fathers worshiped in this mountain; and ye say, that in Jerusalem is the place where men ought to worship" (John 4:20).

These words were spoken by a woman at a well at the foot of Mount Gerizim in Samaria, where Jesus stopped for a drink of water, and reveal a long-standing conflict between the Jews and Samaritans.

Mount Gerizim is the southern member of a pair of mountains, between which lies the site of ancient Shechem. The northern mountain, Ebal, is taller. This is a strategic location since travel routes meet in the pass formed by the mountains. Thus the town of Shechem is frequently mentioned in Genesis. It was on Ebal and Gerizim that the tribes assembled under Joshua to hear the curse and the blessings connected with the violation and observance of the law (Deut. 11:29).

The Samaritans maintained that Shechem, the first capital of Israel, was the place chosen by God for His inhabitation. Jews claimed that God's chosen spot was Jerusalem. Which was the city of God?

Captured by Assyrians in 722 B.C., the city of Samaria became a military colony. The newcomers intermarried with the Samaritans and accepted their religion.

The Persian Empire fell in 333 B.C., and Macedonians under Alexander the Great proceeded down the coast of Syria toward Egypt. Jerusalem was among the cities that surrendered to the Macedonians. In 332 B.C. Samaria revolted, and in punishment Alexander sent Greek colonists there.

When a Greek colony was established, native villages under Greek control often formed a union around an ancestral sanctuary. This is what happened at Shechem. The "Sidonians (Canaanites) of Shechem" were organized in this Greek style to serve the God of Israel. They would neither accept the Macedonians nor become dependents of Jerusalem. They told the Jews, ". . . We seek your God as you do. . ." (Ezra 4:2), but would not give in to the Jews' demands to worship in Jerusalem.

The people of Shechem founded a new sanctuary. Consecrated to the God of both Jerusalem and Shechem, it stood on the summit of Gerizim, overlooking Shechem.

The chief quarrel between Jew and Samaritan was over which possessed the Holy Temple of God. Later each side invented stories of their own to explain the origins of the Samaritan temple controversy. The Samaritans claimed their temple was founded by Alexander the Great. The Jews said it was founded by the son of a high-priestly family, whom Nehemiah expelled from the temple because he had married a Samaritan girl. Claims such as these obscured the real origin of the schism and confused its dating, which is still not clearly known.

---

the prophets, and a benedictory prayer (Megillah 4:3). Only certain persons were permitted to lead in worship, thus Jesus' right to do so was questioned (Mark 6:2-4). Paul taught at synagogues, but he too had some difficulty (Acts 17:17; 26:11).

Jews considered the followers of Jesus to be a party within Judaism. They were therefore allowed to worship on the Sabbath alongside their fellows at the synagogues and temple.

Jesus loved the temple and respected it. He supported it by encouraging His followers to attend it. He declared it to be sacred (Matt. 23:16ff.) and believed it to be worthy of cleansing (Matt. 21:12). Yet Jesus said that "in this place is one greater than the temple" (Matt. 12:6), referring to Himself. He charged that the temple had been turned into a "den of thieves" (Matt. 21:13).

At first, the disciples had conflicting emotions about temple and synagogue worship. Eventually, though, the Jews and Christians antagonized each other so much that there was little choice but to worship separately. This conflict did not revolve around the format or the location of worship, but the nature of worship itself. This is reflected in Jesus' conversation with the Samaritan woman at the well. She said, "Our fathers worshiped in this mountain; and ye say, that in Jerusalem is the place where men ought to worship." She clearly thought of worship in terms of external features, such as the location.

Western Wall, Jerusalem. The holiest shrine in the Jewish world is the western side of the wall that Herod the Great built to enclose his temple area. The wall is called the "Wailing Wall" for two reasons: First, the Jews gather here to mourn the loss of their temple. Furthermore, legend says that the drops of dew that form on the stones are tears shed by the wall in sympathy with the exiled Jews.

Jesus replied, "Woman, believe me, the hour cometh when ye shall neither in this mountain nor yet at Jerusalem, worship the Father . . . But the hour is cometh, and now is, when the true worshipers will worship the Father in spirit and in truth, for the Father seeketh such to worship him" (John 4:21, 23). Christ and His followers knew that salvation and righteousness came not from offerings and sacrifices, but from obeying God in "spirit and in truth." When God acts and we react in worship, our visible reaction is not so important as our invisible attitude. (Perhaps Abel's offering was acceptable because he had no hatred in his heart, while Cain's offering was unacceptable on account of his hatred for his brother.)

We do not know whether Jesus and the apostles participated in all of the Jewish rituals and feasts. The New Testament gives us no complete account of their activities. But there is some evidence that the early Christians gathered in houses for worship, much as the Jews met in local synagogues. Paul refers to "the church in thy house" (Philem. 2), "the church that is in their house" (Rom. 16:5), and "the church which is in his house" (Col. 4:15). Later, under severe Roman persecution, the places of meeting were even more humble and even secretive.

FOOTNOTES

Chapter Three: *"Marriage and Divorce"*

[1]*See* E.A. Speiser, *The Anchor Bible: Genesis* (New York: Doubleday and Company, 1964), pp. 182–185.

[2]Some hold that this phrase—"not under bondage"—means that a deserted Christian spouse may lawfully go from divorce to remarriage. But other scholars question this interpretation.

Chapter Ten: *"Music"*

[1]Maureen W. Barwise, "Hearing the Music of Ancient Egypt," *The Consort,* Vol. 25 (1968–1969), pp. 345–361.

[2]David Wulston, "The Earliest Music Notation," *Music and Letters,* Vol. 52, No. 4 (Oct. 1971), p. 365.

ACKNOWLEDGMENTS

The Publisher gratefully acknowledges the cooperation of these sources, whose illustrations appear in the present work:

Augsburg Publishing House, 140, 148; Bildarchiv Photo Marburg, 52, 72; British Museum, 93, 121, 136, 163, 169; British School of Archaeology, 154, 158; Gaalyah Cornfeld, 153, 178; Department of Museums (Cyprus), 66; Egyptian National Museum, 21; Fototeca Unione, 27; German Archaeological Institute, 44; Giegel (Zurich), 15; Ha-Aretz Museum, 3, 8; Iraq Museum, 37; Levant Photo Service, 112; The Louvre, 34; Israel Government Press Office, 189, 193; Israel Department of Antiquities and Museums, 32, 64, 86, 115, 161, 187; Matson Photo Service, 113, 175, 185; Metropolitan Museum of Art, 165; R. H. Mount, Jr., 176; Thomas Nelson, Inc., 198; Oriental Institute, 85, 156, 166; Reader's Digest Association, 103; Claude Schaeffer-Forrer, 20; Charles Scribner's Sons & B. T. Batsford, Ltd., 151; Standard Publishing Co., 4, 7, 42, 126, 146; University Museum, 24; University of Tel Aviv, 172; A.A.M. Van der Heyden, 97; Howard Vos, 101.

The Publishers have attempted to observe the legal requirements with respect to the rights of the suppliers of photographic materials. Nevertheless, persons who have claims are invited to apply to the Publishers.

INDEX

This index is designed as a guide to proper names and other significant topics, found in *Daily Life In Bible Times*. Page numbers in italics indicate pages where a related illustration or sidebar appears. Headings in italics indicate the title of a book or some other important work of literature. Use the index to find related information in various articles.